COSMOPOLITAN

RAPE: your survival guide

Elizabeth Udall

ROBSON BOOKS

First published in Great Britain in 2003 by Robson Books,
The Chrysalis Building, Bramley Road, London, W10 6SP

A member of **Chrysalis** Books plc

British Library Cataloguing in Publication Data
A catalogue record for this title is available from the British Library.

ISBN 1 86105 622 2

Typeset by FiSH Books, London
Printed by Creative Print & Design (Wales), Ebbw Vale

RAPE:
your
survival
guide

For Mark
Betsy, Joe and Eve

Contents

Acknowledgements

I would like to thank every individual, support group and organisation who has helped me with this book. But I would particularly like to mention Helen Jones, Lynne Harne, Bernie Ryan, Sandra Woodward, everyone at The Haven, Andrew Buckingham, Van Scoyoc, Heather Gay and, of course, Richard Walton. You have all informed, inspired and supported me. Thanks also to Emma Dally and Joanne Brooks for your understanding and guidance. But most of all I want to say thank you to all the women who told me their stories. This book is for you and for every survivor of rape.

Editor's Letter

Each month, as I go through the moving, funny and personal letters from our readers, I am always struck by the huge numbers of young women who write to me about rape. It is a subject in the magazine that produces more response than any other, and these letters are a testament to the enormous importance of this issue in the lives of young women today.

The readers tell me incredibly intimate details of what they have gone through, emotionally and physically. They also write about friends, sisters and sometimes mothers who have been raped. Quite frequently we are asked by very troubled young women if what their boyfriends, male friends or dates have just done to them is really rape. And rape survivors tell me how they feel they suffer twice – once at the hands of their attacker and then again in the arms of the law. Many women (or their relatives) write of how truly awful their experience of taking a rapist to court was, of how humiliated and frightened they were.

To be honest, these letters are heartbreaking and they have moved both me and my team to tears on more than one occasion. The overwhelming message I get from those brave women who write to *Cosmopolitan* is that they welcome every scrap of information and advice we print. They devour every word of our features on rape, be they our first-person interviews or our really practical and well-researched advice features. Those readers' letters prompted us to publish this book.

We were the first publication to highlight the risk of drug rape in this country and we are still campaigning to get all date rape drugs banned. We led the field in demanding that date rape be taken more seriously as a crime and now we are campaigning to set up a 24-hour, seven-day-a-week helpline for women who have been sexually assaulted.

I believe *Cosmopolitan* is the voice of young women on this issue. I don't think it is an exaggeration to say we really know everything there is to know about the subject from a woman's point of view – and we want to share that knowledge. I want you to feel safer on the streets, in bars, clubs, restaurants and at parties. I hope this book will achieve that. We don't want to scare you, we want to reassure you and to give you all the information you need. After all, that is *Cosmo*'s role in society. And do remember we love men at *Cosmo* and want you to going on loving them too. The aim of the book is to respond to all those readers asking for advice, help and sympathy. It's all here for you.

Lorraine Candy, editor, *Cosmopolitan*

Foreword

Rape. It is a four-letter word. It is a word we often avoid using but it is more than just a word. It is something that we know about, something that we fear, but where does our knowledge come from and are our fears justified? Rape is rarely talked about and so our knowledge is largely formed through assumptions and the many myths surrounding rape – that rapists are sex-crazed strangers, that the way women dress and behave provokes men to rape, that rape is a fate worse than death.

This book tackles the myths. It tells the truth about rape. It speaks honestly about the extent and nature of sexual violence in our twenty-first-century society. It speaks to women and to men but it does not do so to raise our fears. It speaks honestly to extend our knowledge. Knowledge is power. Through knowing more about rape we can gain the power to survive sexual violence.

However, although this book speaks to men and women, it is not gender-neutral. It acknowledges that men are raped but it also makes clear that rape is a form of behaviour predominantly conducted by men against women. This does not mean that it talks about women as victims. Women are strong. We need to be! We work, play, study, raise children and we survive discrimination of all kinds, whether through being paid less than our male counterparts, experiencing domestic violence or being raped. Despite differences in personal background, age, ability, geography, class, history or culture, we share the fact that we are women.

Many women have contributed to the making of this book and you will find many accounts of women's experiences of sexual violence. These are powerful because women's voices unite us emotionally; we can all feel the truth of these women's experiences in our own lives and in the lives of our families and friends. Reading about how women survive rape and other forms of sexual violence can help us understand what women need to empower themselves and reclaim their lives.

It is important to note that this book contains practical information and not simply advice. We must remember that rape takes away physical integrity and personal control and that giving advice is just another way of diminishing a woman's control over her own life. Advice is merely telling someone what to do. A woman who has been raped does not need that: what she needs is information about the full range of options available to her. She can then begin to regain control over her own life by making her own decisions. The information contained within this book can aid this process.

This book will be interesting and useful to a wide audience. You may be reading it for yourself or to better understand the experiences of a friend or family member. You may be one of the many women across the country lobbying for changes in the law, campaigning to raise public awareness or establishing and maintaining rape crisis centres. This book can be seen as another step along the path of making sexual violence visible because it is rigorous and unrelenting in its accounting and recounting of rape. For those who prefer the myths rather than the reality, this book will be shocking. For those who have experienced sexual violence, it will be invaluable. Whether your experience was recent or long ago, this book can be seen as a wise and knowledgeable companion that refuses to be silenced.

This book is welcome because it speaks the truth and provides useful, practical information that can help to empower us all. I hope it finds its way into every library, every police station, every rape crisis centre and every home in the country, but, more than that, I hope it is read. Whatever your reason for reading this book I hope you find what you are looking for and realise that you are not alone.

Dr Helen Jones
Rape Crisis Federation of Wales and England

Preface

This book is for all survivors of rape, for those around them and for those of us who fear it.

Rape is a hidden crime. Statistics barely reflect the numbers who have experienced it. Some women talk about it but most do not. Those who choose not to talk are often frightened – frightened of their attacker and frightened of the way they may be treated if they tell anyone. So they remain silent.

Because of this silence, the unrepresentative figures, the limited insight into the reality of this crime, most of us do not realise how many women are being raped. In fact, one in four girls and women will be the victim of rape or attempted rape in their lifetime. Yet we think it will never happen to us. That is what most of the women in this book thought too. But everyone is vulnerable to rape.

There is much we can be aware of in terms of personal safety advice. But whether or not we choose to incorporate that advice into our lives, we are not to be held responsible if we are raped. We should not say, If only I'd done this or If I hadn't done that. Rape is never the fault of those who experience it. It is the fault of the rapist.

These pages largely explore rape from the female perspective and refer to the rapist as male because most rapes are committed by men against women and girls. But there is also acknowledgement that women sexually abuse children and adults and that men rape boys and men. And the book also discusses the male experience of rape and sexual abuse.

The stories here show women choosing to get through the aftermath of rape. Not one is a victim. In the areas of this book dealing with the criminal justice system, the word 'victim' is used. This is because it is the word used by the police and courts, who regard you as a victim of crime. But this book tries not to talk about rape victims. These women are survivors.

Rape is not about sex. Rape is about power. It's about removing control and certainty, about disregarding your wishes and feelings. It's about complete violation of everything that is yours – and then being left to cope with the fallout.

You may be anxious that you could be raped. You may worry about reports of women being raped on holiday or being drug-raped and wonder if there is anything you can do to try to keep yourself safe. Perhaps it is in a relationship that you feel unsafe or even in your own home.

You may have experienced rape and have been left feeling destabilised, confused, hurt. You could be wondering what you should do next, if you should do anything.

But whatever your circumstances, this book can help you.

It is helpful not to read chapters or sections in isolation. There are, of course, areas highlighted that you may feel are particularly relevant to you. But there will certainly also be advice in other parts of the book you may wish to draw on.

As well as being a valuable resource, this book highlights scientific advances, pilot schemes and proposed changes in survivor care and the detection of rape, as well as looking at the huge overhaul in the laws on sex crime currently taking place in this country. This is the future for rape and its survivors.

We need to improve the situation for those survivors and for every woman who fears rape. Public education and the rape conviction rate are key areas but still only two elements of many that need to be addressed if we are to effectively deter rapists from committing this crime.

There is no right way to deal with rape. But this book can show you that there are effective ways to deal with your fears about rape and it will reassure you that if you are a rape survivor, you are far from alone.

The book brings together survivors' experiences, expert advice and opinion and the latest research. And it provides comprehensive information on all forms of support, as well as on forensic medical examinations, police practice and court procedure. All this is intended to help guide you through the personal safety and survival options available to you.

You cannot control everything that happens in your life and that includes being raped. But you can make personal safety choices that could empower you, that might help you avoid or escape rape – whether you face a rapist only once or you face one in your life every day.

And if you have survived rape, remember that you did not choose for it to happen. It was not your fault. No one chooses to be raped, to have their power taken from them. But you can choose what happens next. And this book could give you back some power, could give you the confidence to take your next step.

1

An Introduction

Most of us feel we know about rape – who usually commits it, how a victim reacts afterwards, what the police will do if it's reported and what happens to victims in a rape trial. Or at least we think we do. In fact, research shows that all the ideas we have about rape are based on a set of presumptions that bear little relation to reality.

These presumptions about rape, often referred to as 'rape myths', have far-reaching effects – on victims, on those close to them, the police and the courts. They can affect the survivor's choice to communicate what's happened and even influence whether or not she receives justice.

Professor Liz Kelly is director of the Child and Woman Abuse Studies Unit at London Metropolitan University. She is also author of a review conducted in 2002 on the reporting, investigation and prosecution of rape cases for the Crown Prosecution Service (CPS) and the police inspectorates. In it she quotes one common presumption – that to be raped is worse than being killed, 'or at least one of the most terrible things that can happen'. In fact, she counters, according to research evidence, rape is commonplace 'and most victims choose to survive it'.

Kelly acknowledges that there are some women for whom rape is the ultimate crime. Maybe they were vulnerable to begin with, perhaps they have few resources or they might lack support. In these cases, she says, rape can leave a woman profoundly damaged.

'But experiences of rape and its aftermath are not all the same. Rape is, of course, frightening and invasive. But it is not always devastating.

'Even in situations close to everyone's worst nightmare women can find a way through. And some women say that they are stronger as a consequence of surviving rape. We have to have a more realistic perspective.'

It is the belief in a stereotype – that rape is always by a stranger with a weapon, outside the home, and it is always a woman's worst nightmare – that prevents us from accepting the more mundane reality of rape – that it is sex without the woman's consent, most often with a partner, within their home.

And this is why, in turn, we find rape statistics so shocking – and very often unbelievable. We are told that one in four women and girls will be the victim of rape or attempted rape during their lifetime; we imagine only the stranger-rape scenario and reason it is not possible for that to happen so often.

Many people believe that anything other than the stranger-rape scenario is not 'real rape' and it's important to point out – as obvious as it may seem – that 'people' doesn't only refer to survivors and those around them, it refers to the police, solicitors, barristers and juries, who are people too. And that is why our presumptions, these myths and ideas about what makes a rape 'real', have profound effects.

In order to deal with this, there need to be changes to the law, but there also has to be more emphasis on victim care and public education.

A lot of work clearly needs to be done on attitudes to rape. A 1998 study of young men, 'Young People's Attitudes Towards Violence, Sex and Relationships', showed that they felt it was OK to rape a woman if a man was so turned on he couldn't stop, if he'd spent a lot of money on a woman or if nobody would find out. And there were significant numbers who felt it was acceptable to rape a woman you'd been going out with for a long time or who was your wife.

There are, however, sweeping changes planned to overhaul Britain's sex-crime laws in 2003. And a government action plan is already beginning to implement the recommendations of the 2002 joint report from Her Majesty's Inspectorate of Constabulary and Her Majesty's Crown Prosecution Service into the investigation and prosecution of rape cases, which will, they say, 'be of real benefit to the victims of this repulsive crime'.

There is much that remains to be done, particularly in the areas of public education and support for survivors. But Liz Kelly is nevertheless encouraged. 'There appears currently to be renewed awareness of rape and more commitment to changing the situation in this country for those who choose to report than ever before.'

What is rape?

The current legal definition in England and Wales is simple. Rape is penile penetration of the vagina or anus without consent.

A man commits rape if he has unlawful sexual intercourse with a person if he or she does not consent to it at the time. It is also unlawful if there is a good chance the person doesn't consent to it but the man ignores it. This includes male and female victims and applies whatever the relationship between the people involved.

A 2002 government white paper, 'Protecting the Public', has proposed that the definition of rape be widened to include penetration of the mouth by the penis. It has also proposed that the offence of indecent assault be replaced by two new offences of sexual assault by penetration and sexual assault alone. The former, which would include bottles or objects other than a penis, would carry a life sentence. Non-penetrative assaults, which could also involve high levels of degradation and trauma, will carry a maximum sentence of ten years.

In Scotland

In Scots law rape is described as 'the carnal knowledge of a woman forcibly and against her will'. But all that is necessary is that the victim did not consent to sexual intercourse. Even if there are no signs of violence having been used, a man can still be convicted of rape.

If the woman is drugged in order to overcome her will, the crime is rape. The crime of 'clandestine injury to women' is committed when sexual intercourse is had with a woman who is not conscious through sleep, a fit, drink or the like 'so that she neither yields nor withholds consent'.

A husband may be guilty of raping his wife whether or not he is living with her.

It is not rape for a man to have forcible anal or oral intercourse with a female victim. Such an offence is indecent assault. Equally, a male person cannot be raped by another man, or by a woman. Penetration of the vagina is essential for rape but it need not be complete penetration.

There is no presumption or rule that because a boy is under the age of puberty (fourteen years of age) he can't, in law, commit rape. Any person who has unlawful sexual intercourse with any girl under the age of thirteen years commits an offence, the maximum punishment of which is life imprisonment.

In Northern Ireland

In Northern Ireland the legal definition of rape is penetration of the labia by the penis (no matter how slight) committed by a man on a woman who is not his wife, if she has not given consent or is unable to give consent. A man may also be found guilty if the woman's response to the prospect of sex was ambiguous and he failed to obtain a clear response.

This definition does not include anal rape and oral rape. Present legislation does not recognise that both men and boys can be raped. In such cases charges of indecent assault or buggery are brought. Penetration with objects and weapons is regarded as indecent assault, with a maximum penalty of ten years' imprisonment.

The charge of unlawful carnal knowledge, commonly referred to as statutory rape, recognises that girls of between the ages of fourteen and seventeen may agree to have sex, while the law does not regard them as being able to give informed consent until they are seventeen. When teenage boys rape girls, they are generally charged with unlawful carnal knowledge. This is a less serious offence with less severe penalties.

How many women are raped?

For the past thirty years, the number of women reporting rape has increased steadily and in recent years has risen dramatically. In the year 2001–2 there were 9,008 reported rapes on women and 735 on men. But numerous studies, as well as figures from support groups, show that these figures indicate only a fraction of the number of rapes that actually take place.

The British Crime Survey measures the amount of crime in England and Wales by asking people about crimes they have experienced in the last year. It includes crimes that are not reported to the police. And their most recent figures for rape, in 2000, showed figures nearly ten times those recorded by the police.

British Crime Survey figures are therefore closer to the real numbers of women being raped. But it should be stressed that even these will be underestimates. This means that, according to the 2000 Survey, there were a minimum of 61,000 women, aged over sixteen, being raped every year at the end of the 1990s.

Rape risk factors

The British Crime Survey found that women being raped outside by a stranger with a weapon was the least likely scenario. Most women are raped by their partners, inside their home. And because these close relationships provide opportunities for other types of coercion – for example emotional or financial – weapons are not necessarily needed.

The Home Office say that age is the biggest single risk factor for experiencing all kinds of sexual victimisation. Women aged between 16 and 24 were significantly more likely to say they had been victimised than older women. Higher than average risks were also reflected by single women, students and women from privately rented households. But it is likely that this reflects the same pattern as age, as large numbers of young women are found in these groups.

The myths surrounding rape

A conviction is more likely when the facts of the case match the classic picture of a stranger rape, that is, one committed by someone the woman has never met, outside and using a weapon. But, as has already been mentioned, as the majority of rapes are committed by someone known to the victim and take place inside, the facts rarely fit this stereotype. Yet because the women who are raped by strangers are more likely to report to the police and their cases are more likely to go to trial and result in a conviction – and these are the rape cases we hear about – the stereotype is perpetuated.

The myths – and the reality

*Failing to struggle does not mean a woman wanted it. A woman can freeze for fear of her life, for the safety of someone close to her or because she's been threatened with a weapon. Men are also generally stronger than women so they might use physical coercion. And if it's someone she knows he may well rely on psychological coercion. A rapist might also use drugs, including alcohol, to render a woman incapable of responding in any way at all. But without any form of coercion, rape is still an act of violence. It is sex forced on a woman against her will.

*Women don't say 'No' when they mean 'Yes'. Many people still believe that it is wrong for women to want sex and, if they do, they should feel guilty about it They think that women play hard to get because they are struggling with their guilt and that secretly they fantasise about rape – they even require a degree of force to achieve sexual arousal. This is WRONG. When a woman says 'No' she means 'No'.

*'Nice' girls do get raped. There is no typical victim. Women of all ages and from all classes and ethnic backgrounds are raped.

*Women don't 'ask for it' by wearing certain clothes or behaving in a certain way or being in the wrong place. Rape is ALWAYS the rapist's fault.

*Men do not get 'taken over' by a sexual urge they can't control. They can control it. And rape isn't about sex. It's about violence and power.

*Rapists are not usually 'madmen'. Few rapists are sent for psychiatric treatment. Many rapists appear normal. Often they have steady jobs and relationships with wives or girlfriends. The police interviewed Peter Sutcliffe nine times before they discovered that he was the Yorkshire Ripper. He didn't fit their image of a mass rapist and murderer because he was married, had a steady job and a nice home.

*'She made it up.' Only 2 per cent of rape allegations are false. This is the same number as for all other crimes.

*Rape does not usually happen at the hands of a stranger, with a weapon, outside, at night. Rape can happen at any time of day, it mostly happens inside, and the rapist is usually a man known to the woman.

Providing support

Most rape survivors will have a support group in their area on which they can call. Some groups are local, other organisations operate nationally; they might work independently or as part of another service, for example, as counselling in sexual-assault referral centres (SARCs).

Services can include telephone helplines, face-to-face counselling, and advocacy and/or chaperone services for victims reporting to the police or going to court.

But not every survivor will have a group close to them. And this is not necessarily only the case in rural areas. 'For example, there are no centres in Leeds or Birmingham. It's a geographical lottery,' says Lynne Harne, press officer of the Rape Crisis Federation

The Rape Crisis Federation was established in 1996 and acts as a central referral service for individuals seeking help, provides minimum standards for rape crisis groups, raises public awareness of the issues and supports campaigns to end rape and gain justice for victims.

The 45 groups that form the Federation receive over 50,000 calls a year. But there is a vast variation in the provision of service. The central office receives Home Office funding but individual services receive no statutory funding. Some areas operate only with trained volunteers.

'The rape crisis groups in the Federation are hugely under-resourced,' says Lynne Harne. 'Some local centres are better funded and are supported by their local authorities. But most struggle constantly with funding and a few have been forced to shut down altogether. This is despite the fact that there is increasing public recognition of the support needed for victims of rape and that new government legislation will encourage more women to seek help in reporting assaults.

'Helplines are under-staffed so they cannot provide a round-the-clock response. Some are open until ten at night, others only in the day. But some women want immediate support – and may give up if they cannot get help soon after the rape.

'Our eventual aim is to be able to offer a national, 24-hour, seven-day-a-week telephone helpline,' says Harne. 'But at the moment that is just not possible because of lack of funding.'

The Rape and Sexual Assault Support Centre (RASASC) in south London provides the only 365-days-a-year rape crisis helpline in the country. From July 2003 it will be offering face-to-face counselling and from November 2003 an advocacy service for women wanting to report to the police and go to court. But these extra services would not have been possible without the funding they were awarded by the Association of London Government in 2002.

'We are extremely grateful,' says Yvonne Traynor, the centre's service director. 'But what seems like a massive lump sum actually has to last us four years. We've also had to make applications to other funders, which we're waiting to hear about.

'Securing funding really is an uphill struggle. We just want to get on with the work we are here for without worrying about money.'

'But the majority of local groups are able to offer a confidential telephone helpline service some days and/or evenings a week,' says Lynne Harne. 'And although there may be a waiting list, many groups can provide face-to-face counselling for survivors.

'And survivors with no crisis centre nearby can access counselling services from a centre in a town nearest to where they live. They can also get support and advice from a confidential helpline telephone service from any group in the country. It does not have to be their local one.'

But Liz Kelly feels there is a crucial area of support that has largely been ignored. 'Most women tell their friends when they've been raped,' says Kelly. 'And we certainly haven't done enough work to enable friends and families to be effective supporters of rape survivors.' (See Chapter 8 for information on supporting survivors.)

The cases lost along the way

In 1977, one in three reported cases of rape resulted in a conviction for rape. This has now dropped dramatically to one in thirteen.

When cases are lost during the criminal justice process, up to the time the case reaches court, it is called attrition. This has been increasing for more than twenty years and is a key area of concern for policy makers. They want to know why women are withdrawing their allegations and why so many cases are not reaching trial, let alone ending in conviction.

Where are cases being lost?

The majority of cases are lost at the beginning because most women don't report rape.

At the next stage, of initial response and investigation, which includes reporting to the police, forensic examination, statement taking, evidence gathering and arrest and/or interviewing of the suspect, half the cases are lost in the UK. This can happen for a number of reasons, including:

*failure to identify or find the suspect

*designation of the case as a false report

*victim withdrawal

*police decisions to take no further action

The third stage consists of the referral of a case to the Crown Prosecution Service (CPS), which has been criticised for looking for reasons *not* to continue with cases, rather than seeking positive areas on which it can build. At this point, between a third and a half of referred cases are either discontinued or the charges are reduced.

Of the rape cases that reach trial, only half result in a conviction for rape or attempted rape. A third to a quarter result in acquittals. The remaining cases involve convictions for charges other than rape.

Many studies show that rape victims describe giving evidence in court as like becoming a victim all over again. This leaves them feeling disillusioned with the criminal justice system, particularly if they believe their attacker has been wrongly acquitted.

What is changing?

There have been key developments over the last twenty years, not least the Court of Appeal case *R vs. R*, which set the precedent in 1991 that a man could no longer legally rape his wife. This was written into law in 1994. Also in 1994, the 1956 Sexual Offences Act was amended by the Criminal Justice and Public Order Act to include non-consensual intercourse between men.

It was in 1998 that comprehensive change became a realistic prospect with the publication of a Cabinet Office policy paper entitled 'Living Without Fear'. This paper expressed concern for the numbers of rape cases being lost in the criminal justice process and contained proposals for the complete overhaul of sexual offences. In her 2002 review for the CPS and police inspectorates, Liz Kelly points out that it represented the 'first official government statement on violence against women in England and Wales'.

'Living Without Fear' was followed, two years later, by 'Setting the Boundaries', a Home Office report which was critical of the investigation and prosecution of rape allegations.

It made eighteen recommendations and called for these proposed changes to become a countrywide priority.

It was on the basis of the joint police and CPS report on rape that the government formulated an action plan in 2002. Later the same year, a white paper, 'Protecting the Public', proposed the first overhaul for more than a hundred years of the laws on rape, child abuse and incest.

The Sexual Offences Bill was introduced in the Lords in January 2003. At the time of writing, the bill is on the verge of becoming law. It is hoped that these changes will help to give women the confidence to report rape and to go through the trial process.

Improvements in rape reporting and investigation
Negative expectations of police response feature as a key factor in the reasons rape survivors give for not reporting the crime. But the most recent study to explore police response found that most victims were positive about it.

The Metropolitan Police Force's Project Sapphire is claimed to be the most comprehensive reform of rape investigation ever undertaken by the police. But it has been argued that the Met is the only service so far to have made rape a priority. However, there are many forces who have moved rape further up their agendas.

Several forces across the country have been instrumental in the establishment of sexual-assault referral centres (SARCs). These centres work closely with the police in their areas, often providing training for them in the care of victims of sex crime.

The country now has six sexual-assault referral centres in London, Tyneside and Northumberland, Leicestershire, Yorkshire, Lancashire and Manchester. St Mary's Sexual Assault Referral Centre in Manchester has been a pioneer in this approach to care and was cited in the influential 2000 Home Office report 'Setting the Boundaries' as a model of best practice. And there are plans for three more such centres – one in Cambridgeshire and two more in London.

These centres have pioneered self-referral, enabling women to obtain support and medical examination independently of the police. Evidence from an examination can be gathered and stored, giving the victim the option of reporting at a later date, knowing the evidence has not been lost. She might also choose to make an anonymous report to the police. It is hoped that innovations such as these not only improve choices for, and care of, survivors but that they might also increase reporting to the police.

There are pilot schemes to train nurses to carry out forensic examinations in order to deal with the current problems in the numbers and availability of female doctors, which can lead to long waits for victims. There are new guidelines for all medical examiners, which aim to standardise and improve evidence-gathering and there is a 'first-response kit', which is now available for police officers to capture early evidence. It is hoped all these measures will benefit survivors, in terms of their care and in the detection of, and consequently the conviction rate for, rape.

Sympathetic and expert treatment from the outset, such as that found at SARCs, or from other sources, like the police, should send out a message to women that their complaints will be taken seriously.

Improvements in case referral to prosecutors
In response to evidence that, of the few cases reaching referral to prosecutors, large numbers of those are being lost, the government has put forward plans for a network of specialist prosecutors. It has also proposed that these prosecutors seek a second opinion on decisions to drop cases or reduce charges. Liz Kelly is encouraged by this. 'Specialist prosecutors developing skills and knowledge around rape will enable them to have a better sense of what

additional evidence might be helpful and can only be a step forward.'

Improvements in court

To tackle the frighteningly low conviction rate – the total number of men being found guilty of rape and cautioned in 2000 was only 594 or 7 per cent of those cases reported – the government has announced far-reaching reforms of the laws on sex crime.

In the white paper, 'Protecting the Public', reforms planned to strengthen legislation around rape include a tighter definition of what amounts to consent to sex. Speaking in November 2002, the Home Secretary, David Blunkett, commented, 'We want to assume that if someone makes love they do so with free agreement, not that they are forced to or conned into it.'

The tougher laws are intended to limit the numbers of accused men, having convinced juries that they honestly believed their victims agreed to sex, who walk free as a result.

Other measures being considered include challenging offensive, but not necessarily relevant, questioning of alleged rape victims in court, for example, inappropriate cross-examination about previous sexual experience. There are also plans to allow courts to study not only evidence of an alleged rapist's previous convictions but also his acquittals. This means that if the alleged rapist has been in court for the same or a similar offence in the past, even if he wasn't convicted, this can be taken into account. Former witnesses could be called to give evidence in the new case.

'The white paper is making a difference purely by what it represents,' says Liz Kelly. 'Sex-offences legislation will no longer be based on nineteenth-century understandings, but on what we know now. In the twenty-first century, sex has to be about free agreement between two people, that it is something both of them want on each occasion.'

What the changes mean for rape survivors

It is hoped that the improved profile of rape issues, through changes in practice, in policy and in the law, will have a favourable effect on the provision of support services for rape survivors and on public education. 'Rape is higher on the public agenda than it ever has been,' says Lynne Harne of the Rape Crisis Federation.

No one thing will make a difference. But, if we can address the gaps in overall response to supporting survivors and in public education, that in turn will support the legal reforms. And together these changes will begin to alter the public's perception of, and its attitude to, rape.

2

Sexual Abuse in Childhood

As children we are encouraged to believe we can trust the adults in our lives and taught we should do what they ask. But some adults exploit this trust to abuse a child sexually.

There is no specific legal offence of 'child sex abuse' so, as such, there is no official legally recognised definition of an offence. But the Home Office defines it as any activity with a child under the age of sixteen, whether or not the child agrees to it, that a reasonable person would consider to be sexual or indecent.

Over half the calls to the Rape Crisis Federation's member groups in 2001 – 56 per cent – were from girls and women who were survivors of childhood sexual abuse. This reflects the large number of calls being received by all rape support services. There are also many groups specifically for adult survivors of rape and sexual abuse in childhood who are overwhelmed with calls. This is testament to the numbers of people experiencing this crime and to its profound and long-term effects. But, when it is considered that studies have shown that the majority of survivors of child sexual abuse tell no one, there is some indication of the real extent of this problem.

Research shows that one in two women will experience some form of sexual abuse – from flashing to rape – before her eighteenth birthday, one-third before she is twelve. A 2001 *Cosmopolitan* sex crime survey found that a third of women had experienced sexual assault when they were younger than sixteen.

Abuse may only happen once but it is more likely to be a frequent occurrence over an extended period of time. And it has been found that in nearly two-thirds of cases children suffered from abuse from their own family.

According to 'Childhood Matters', the report of the National Commission Inquiry into the Prevention of Child Abuse in May 1997, at least half of the abuse that occurs, sometimes over lengthy periods of a child's life, remains undisclosed at the time of occurrence. Cambridge Rape Crisis Centre and Cleveland Rape and Sexual Abuse Counselling Service point out that up to 80 per cent of all sexual assaults against children go unreported.

If cases are reported, many go down the civil child-protection route. But, of the child-sexual-abuse instances where the charges are rape and they go through the criminal justice system, cases are more likely to go forward and result in convictions than in the case of an adult rape. A Home Office research study in 2000, 'Aspects of Crime: Children as Victims', shows that where the age of the child can be identified, the proportion of adults sentenced to an immediate custodial sentence for rape of a female under sixteen was 97 per cent.

Sexual abuse can cause extensive external and internal damage as well as lasting emotional trauma and these things can affect every aspect of someone's life. It takes a great deal of courage to reveal the abuse. Some survivors remember in detail, others simply know that 'something happened'. Some will have 'forgotten' and it is only as adults that their memories resurface. But remembering is often the first step in the healing process.

The control and power that the adult removes from the child has to be regained for an adult survivor to heal. 'If you're a survivor of sexual abuse it becomes your whole life. It becomes you,' says Lucia Hall, a therapist specialising in trauma and abuse. 'That's why it's so important to get professional help. In order to heal your whole world view, which has been created around those incidents, that view has to be shattered and your life rebuilt. You need someone with expertise to take you through that therapeutic process.'

Who does it?

The most common sexual abusers of children are natural fathers, followed by other male family members, such as brothers, uncles and grandfathers, stepfathers and stepbrothers. It may be a trusted family friend, an adult or young person of the same sex – mothers and aunts or a child who's the same age. But many reports suggest that over 95 per cent of offenders are male, that 97 per cent of male attackers are heterosexual and a large proportion are married with children.

What might you have experienced?

Some children experience sexual abuse in isolation from other abuse while some will also be subjected to other physical cruelty, neglect and/or emotional abuse.

Sexual abuse includes touching the genitals and/or masturbating a child; asking the child to touch the genitals and/or masturbate an adult or adults or other children; taking obscene photographs of children; making a child watch or read pornography; performing oral sex on a child or making them perform oral sex on adults or other children; penetration or attempted penetration of the child's vagina or anus with objects, fingers or a penis; being licked or kissed in sexual ways or involving children in prostitution.

What might have been said to you

An abuser will use a number of tactics to persuade children to do what they ask. They might use emotional blackmail, bribery or flattery – 'This is our secret.' They could convince the child that the abuse is a normal way for an adult to express love to a child or they could use threats. 'I'll be sent to prison if you tell,' or 'You'll be taken away from us.' The threats might also be physical, against the child or someone close to them. They might involve a child in an abusive situation, in games or other children may even be used to encourage them to comply. An abuser might even manipulate a child to the point where they initiate contact with the adult.

In a two-year study, paedophiles themselves told Kidscape, the national charity that teaches children how to keep safe before they become victims of abuse, how they ensnare children. They said they:

*tricked children into trusting them

*offered to teach them games, sports or how to play a musical instrument

*took them on outings

*gave them gifts, bribes, toys, money or treats

They often target single-parent families, where mothers might be especially grateful for help with looking after the children – nearly half of paedophiles found their victims through babysitting. And they hang around places that children are likely to frequent.

Kidscape found that around a third of the paedophiles had each committed offences against 10 to 450 children, and almost three-quarters of them against 1 to 10 victims.

Francesca

I don't know when my dad started abusing me. I can't remember it not going on. It never felt right and I knew I didn't like it but it wasn't until high school that I really realised what was going on. I was eleven when it became penetrative. When I was younger he would say he loved me, that I was special. But when I started asking questions he'd say the family would split, that my sister and I would be taken away. And of course I didn't want that to happen. I told a friend what was going on but she didn't believe me. That put me off telling anyone else. Dad had told me no one would believe me so it just confirmed it for me. Mum knew about it. I'd scream the house down when it was happening and I always expected at some point she'd come and rescue me, that she'd find a way to make it stop, but she didn't. I learnt to shut off, like I was somewhere else, when it happened and that helped me cope.

I was nearly seventeen when I told a teacher at school. I felt backed into a corner. I know now that social services had investigated my mum and dad a couple of years earlier. I'd had a lot of gynaecological problems and my doctor had passed on his concerns to them. But nothing came of it. As soon as I admitted what was going on to my teacher I felt my world would fall apart – everything Dad had said would happen was about to. By the time a policewoman arrived at school to talk to me the next day I denied everything. It took most of the day but eventually I admitted it again. When I got home that night they'd already arrested my dad. My sister couldn't stop crying and my mum was so angry. She said, 'How could you break up the family and destroy your sister?' I had a medical examination and my dad was charged with rape and assault of a minor. He was released on bail and stayed with his brother until my sister and I were taken into care – then he went home again.

Two days after I'd made my statement I sat my GCSEs. I passed twelve and went to college for my A levels. My dad constantly turned up at college, pleading with me to withdraw my statement. I felt under so much pressure that I developed an eating disorder. I asked the police if I could retract but they put pressure on me not to. I ended up taking an overdose. I had been in care for eighteen months when the Crown Prosecution Service accepted the case. I was told how hard it would be. There was medical evidence of abuse but it wasn't tied to my dad. The chances of him going to prison were slim. I thought, Why am I doing this? Why am I putting myself through all this? But I didn't want my sister or someone else to go through what I had. I couldn't have lived with myself.

I was eighteen when I went to court. It was hard to take the stand and answer questions with my dad there. I felt so guilty. He was still my dad. I tried not to look at him but his defence barrister stood so I could see him. My dad got a suspended sentence due to lack of evidence. But they did stop him having contact with anyone under eighteen on his own and my sister was left on the child-protection list. I felt it had all been a waste of time. Everything was in ruins. I fell apart. I stopped going to work. Eventually I did odd jobs and after three years of putting it off, feeling I was useless and would never be any good at anything, at 21 I started my degree.

I'm studying for a PhD and am now 26. I'm also engaged to be married. When I first got together with Neil I wouldn't let him near me, even to hold my hand. The feelings still surface sometimes, even now.

I still feel guilty and sad that things turned out as they did. Why couldn't my dad and I have had a normal relationship? Why did he feel he had to hurt me? I've changed my name and moved house now. I needed to start again. Despite everything, I'm glad I reported. I feel it's helped me – that I've done all I could. I know there's a long way to go but I'm getting there slowly.

What have you felt since?

Because it is most likely that child abuse happens over a long period of time, as an adult you may not connect its effects to the abuse.

You may be dealing with a lot of anger and resentment. For example, your education might have been neglected so you performed less well than you could have done if you had not been abused. Perhaps you tried to tell people about the abuse, or knew others were aware of it, but you were not believed, you were rejected or the abuse was ignored.

As a result, perhaps you believe you do not deserve to be treated with care and respect. You might think it was something about you that caused the abuse.

Your sexuality has not been allowed to develop naturally. You will have had to deal with feelings that you were perhaps too young to understand. You might have found some of the abuse physically pleasurable and this could make you feel guilty. But this only means your genitals were functioning properly.

You may have approached your abuser after the initial abuse so now you feel it's unfair to say it was his fault or that he should be punished. But children need affection, so, if this was the only affection you got, then it is understandable that you would have taken it, even sought it, and enjoyed it.

You may now cling to people, desperate for the love and approval you never got as a child. And perhaps you put the needs of others before your own, believing you don't deserve to have your needs considered. Or you may now think sex is the only way you can get attention or believe your only value is sexual, so you seek sex to get those needs met.

Perhaps you now have trouble forming relationships. The thought of sex may repulse you. You may have flashbacks of the abuse during sex or feel numb during the experience because switching off was how you coped during your abuse as a child. Or maybe you might experience sexual pleasure but it reminds you of the arousal you experienced at the time of the abuse – and that makes you feel guilty.

But remember, you have no reason to feel guilty. The sexual abuse you experienced was not your fault.

Steph

I was raped at thirteen by a stranger, a man much older than me, when I was walking home from a friend's house. He grabbed me by my arm and pulled me through a gate. He slammed my head against a tree and the next moment I was on the ground being raped by him. But at the time I had no idea what he was doing. I struggled and threw stones and dirt in his face and when it finished managed to get up.

But he pushed me down and did it again. I thought I was going to die. He banged my head on the ground so much that I was going in and out of consciousness. It was a blur of pain, panic, incomprehension . . . and of just floating, like my mind was trying to protect me from the horror by taking me somewhere else. The next thing, I was at home in the bath with no idea how I'd got there. My memories returned in dribs and drabs. I developed anorexia and attempted suicide. The professionals I saw suspected I had been raped but when they told my parents they were so devastated I couldn't admit they'd been right.

I now have bulimia and I self-harm. I'm 23 and I've married my childhood sweetheart. He was my first sexual relationship after the attack. We've been married five years but now sleep in separate rooms. He's so supportive but I can't cope. The relationship's in tatters. I feel I lost everything – my virginity, my innocence, my childhood, my chance at making a success of a relationship – because of that man. I'm starting to find my voice now but wonder if it's too late. If I'd told just one person and not put it all in a box and rammed the lid on, my life could have been so different.

What can you do now?

You may not want to do anything but if you feel you do then there are many options open to you. It can help to tell at least one other person – at least initially. Experts stress that secrecy and silence are part of the abuse.

Remember you have survived so far, so you have a great deal of strength. Somebody else might be able to help you acknowledge that strength, explore your options and take the first step in coming to terms with your abuse. Someone you might like to think about talking to might be another survivor, a member of a support group, a counsellor, a caring partner or family member or a sibling who also suffered abuse. The ideal is to have a combination of support.

Once you have decided you want to heal, you will move through various stages – knowing it wasn't your fault, grief, anger and moving on.

Male survivors

Survivors UK, the only national organisation that provides support and resources for men who have experienced any form of sexual violence, say that 5 to 10 per cent of boys are sexually abused. 'Two out of three of our callers were abused as children,' says Adam Chugg, the organisation's national co-ordinator. 'And more men were abused from within the family than from outside.'

Men who have experienced abuse as children might have fears and doubts about their sexuality. If they are gay they may feel their sexuality was determined by their experience or that their sexuality made them a target for the abuser, that the abuser 'sensed' they were gay.

Heterosexual men who have survived child sexual abuse can become homophobic because they believe their abusers were gay, that that is why they abused. But research shows that most abusers are heterosexual.

Straight men might also fear they are secretly gay because of physical responses or arousal they experienced during their abuse as children. Because arousal in men is so visibly obvious, male survivors often feel high levels of guilt and shame because the abuser used their physical responses against them.

It is also common for male adult survivors to fear that they will become abusers. But the vast majority of male survivors of sexual abuse do not and being a survivor is never grounds for an abuser to justify his actions.

(See also pages 77–83 for more on adult male rape.)

What is changing?

The overhaul of sex-crime law proposed by the government, in response to recommendations in the 2000 Home Office report 'Setting the Boundaries', is intended to provide better protection against sexual abuse, particularly of children. Under the proposals:

*Children under thirteen will not be capable in law of consent and any sexual intercourse will be treated as rape.

*Cases involving children aged thirteen to sixteen will be covered by the new law against an adult committing a sex act with a child, which carries a fourteen-year sentence.

*A grooming offence will apply to those who 'groom' children for abuse. The accused will have had to have met the child in person.

*A new civil order will ban adults deemed to present a risk from sending explicit emails to children or hanging around playgrounds.

Home Secretary David Blunkett said in November 2002 that Home Office research showed that some violent offenders had a greater propensity to commit sex crimes. 'We are not prepared to wait until they do before we take action,' he said. 'For that reason we will allow sex-offender orders and restraining orders to be taken out against anyone convicted of a serious violent offence if the police believe they present a real risk.'

Proposals also include tackling paedophile use of the Internet and ensuring that incest covers stepparents. It is also expected that a specific offence of persistent child abuse will be created as well as a new crime of 'adult activity with a child'. This would be the first of its kind anywhere in the world and would replace seven different offences that are currently used to prosecute in child-abuse cases and that each carry different age limits and penalties. It would state clearly that some cases of child abuse and paedophilia are so serious that they will in future carry a life sentence.

Is it ever too late to report?

'Setting the Boundaries' recommended that 'there should be no time limits to hinder prosecution of adult sexual abuse of a child'.

'Many people leave it years, sometimes decades, before reporting abuse or sexual assault,' says Richard Walton, head of the Metropolitan Police's Project Sapphire. 'Victims of abuse as children are often vulnerable to sexual assault as adults because they have not received counselling and help. It is vital to get help as soon as possible and it is never too late to seek help, even if the abuse was many years ago.'

Lynne Harne of the Rape Crisis Federation says,'If an adult female survivor of child sex abuse wishes to report to the police we will say that she needs to recognise that it may be difficult to bring a prosecution at this stage. But we will support her in whatever she chooses to do.'

In May 2002, a former army chef, Tony Jasinskyj, was jailed for life for the murder and rape of fourteen-year-old Marion Crofts, more than twenty years earlier. DNA from semen on Marion's clothing matched that taken from him after Jasinskyj, now 45, was arrested in 2001 on suspicion of an assault on his second wife, Michelle. He was jailed for life for murder and ten years for rape, to run concurrently.

Marion had been cycling from her home in Fleet, Hampshire, to band practice at Wavell School, North Camp, Farnborough, on the morning of Saturday, 6 June 1981, when she was attacked. Marion's sister Sally said, after the verdict: 'Today marks the end of 21 years of agony for our family.' And her other sister, Shirley, added, 'We're grateful that Marion's killer has been brought to justice.'

What other action could I take?

Aside from criminal action, a survivor of childhood sexual abuse can make a claim for compensation from the Criminal Injuries Compensation Authority (CICA), or make a civil claim against the person or persons who abused them, or against the organisation who was responsible for that person. There are time limits on these forms of action but this should not discourage anyone from attempting to make a claim.

Tracey Storey, who is a senior solicitor specialising in historical child-abuse cases for Russell, Jones and Walker in London, says that most of the people she sees are in their thirties and forties. 'It is only at that point in their life that many adult survivors of child sexual abuse feel able to speak out. People often feel extreme fear, distress and shame about disclosing abuse.

'The first thing I ask clients who come to see me is if they have reported to the police. This is because the police have greater resources to investigate the crime and to see if anyone else has been involved with the alleged abuser.

'People want to see their abusers brought to justice, even it means going through the ordeal of giving evidence and the possibility of not being believed.

'If the case reaches a criminal court it needs to be proved beyond reasonable doubt that you were abused by this person. This can be hard to do if a lot of time has elapsed – and the low conviction rate reflects this. But there are convictions.'

When you apply for compensation from the CICA, says Storey, the standard of proof is only on the balance of probabilities. 'This means it can be possible to reach a conclusion in your favour, whether or not you secured a conviction in court.'

Normally there is a time limit of two years on applying to the CICA but if you are a victim of violent crime – and the authority defines child sexual abuse as a violent crime – then it will allow late claims. 'They understand that it can take time for survivors to come forward,' says Storey.

You might also wish to consider filing a civil claim. If someone is making a claim against another individual, then there is generally a strict six-year time limit from the person's eighteenth birthday. However, there are exceptions. 'If you were psychologically damaged by your abuse to the point where you were too unwell to make a claim within that time limit, then you may have a case,' Storey explains.

'If you are making a claim that involves an institution – against a local authority in charge of a children's home or school or against the church, for instance – then I say that there is a three-year extendable time limit. There is more flexibility.'

And the majority of civil claims settle out of court once evidence has been compiled, says Storey. 'There have been many, many successful civil actions.

'Compensation is never enough to make up for a lost childhood. But for most of my clients money is not the motivation anyway. It's about getting some sort of acknowledgement for what happened to them and about taking steps to ensure it will never happen again. Compensation can be a way for survivors to make a fresh start by finally being believed, after years of trying to deal with the trauma alone. It can be therapeutic in itself.'

If you want more advice on taking criminal or civil action, contact the Association of Child Abuse Lawyers, who will put you in touch with a lawyer in your area (See page 211).

A woman, who sued a local authority for letting her stay with her abusive father and then failing to protect her from being sexually molested by a children's home employee, settled her

*case in October 2002 for £55,790 at the High Court in London.
The London borough of Southwark agreed the settlement with
the 34-year-old woman.*

Supporting an adult survivor

Listen, believe and help them to investigate their options.
Support whatever decision the survivor makes – even if that is
to do nothing. You may want to make decisions, to encourage
her to seek help because you are worried. But all this will do is
to reinforce her feelings of lack of control in her life. However
much you care, she is the only one who knows what her needs
are. Seek help only if she is suicidal. Ask her about her needs
and how you can help her meet them. But only make offers
and commitments you know you can stick by.

If it's your partner who is seeking your support, tell him or her
that it's OK to say 'No' to sex. Reassure them that their value
to you is more than sexual. If they want sexual interaction, let
them control it by only doing what they feel comfortable with.
Offer non-sexual forms of physical intimacy – holding hands,
massage, hugging. And don't forget to seek help for yourself.

You believe a young person you know is at risk or is a victim

Kidscape and the National Society for the Protection of Cruelty
to Children (NSPCC) suggest some changes in behaviour you
should be aware of and ways you can respond. These signs
do not necessarily mean a child has been abused but they may
help you recognise that something is wrong. The child:

*is overly affectionate or knowledgeable in a sexual way
inappropriate to the child's age

*compulsively masturbates

*suddenly draws explicit pictures

*re-enacts abuse on objects or with other children or adults *becomes worried or panics if you try to remove their clothing

*demonstrates other extreme reactions such as depression, self-mutilation, suicide attempts, running away, compulsively washing, overdoses, anorexia; compulsively eats or suddenly loses appetite

*has physical illness such as stomach ache, headache, general pain

*has personality changes such as becoming insecure or clinging

*regresses to younger behaviour patterns, such as thumb sucking or bringing out discarded cuddly toys

*is isolated or withdrawn

*is fearful of people or places

*is unable to concentrate

*displays a lack of trust or fear of someone they know well, such as not wanting to be alone with a babysitter or child minder

*starts to wet again, day or night

*has nightmares

*tries to be ultra-good or perfect

*overreacts to criticism

*bursts into tears, becomes extremely irritable, bad tempered, full of rage at everyone

Ask, Is someone making you unhappy? Are you afraid of something? Have you got a problem at home or at school? Is someone bullying you? The answer may be 'no' at first. But if you are concerned, ask again.

Medical problems to be aware of include: chronic itching, pain in the genitals, venereal diseases. Ensure the child has a full medical examination with a doctor trained to work with children and who is experienced in dealing with children who have been abused.

A child tells you that he or she is being abused

Give the child all the time he or she wants to talk. The child might tell you a little at a time to test your reaction. He or she may have been threatened or be concerned about your feelings, or that you will not love them or that you will be angry with them about what has happened.

Attempt to stay calm and try not to transmit anger, shock or embarrassment. Accept what the child says without judgements or recriminations. 'If only you hadn't...' types of comment will only make things worse.

Take what is said seriously. Children rarely lie about sexual abuse. Reassure the child. Listen but try not to press the child for information. Say that your are glad they told you.

If the child is angry, sad, fearful, feeling guilty, acknowledge these are natural feelings but keep telling them they are not to blame and they will not be punished. Say you'll keep them safe and do all you can to help. Try not to keep discussing the assault or your feelings about the offender in front of the child.

If the child was sexually abused by someone of the same gender, they might feel 'gay'. You will need to reassure them that being abused doesn't make them homosexual or lesbian. If a boy has been abused by a woman, the experience can be dismissed by some people who say he was 'lucky'. It is still abuse and he will need reassurance and counselling. Praise him for getting through the ordeal.

Your own feelings and reactions are all normal. But if the child feels you are too upset, they may stop talking about it to avoid hurting you more, so try to keep your feelings away from them. And don't impose your views on the child. They may still like or even love their abuser while you hate them.

But they will need to come to terms with the abuse in their own way.

You may find it difficult to report the incident. You may feel guilty that you have failed to protect the child. Others may say, 'You must have known. How could you let that happen?' Remember the abuse is the fault of the child's abuser. It's more productive to ask, How can we make this better? But if something you did put the child at greater risk, change it. Check and re-check the people you leave your child with. And if you were involved with drugs or alcohol and this made you less aware of what was happening, get help.

If the abuser is a partner or close relative you might doubt it has happened – 'I know him. He couldn't have done this.' If action is taken it can cause rifts in the family and if the abuser goes to prison it could cause financial problems for you. You might even feel jealous that your partner focused his sexual attention on the child and then guilt that you should have such feelings. You may love the abuser and just want the abuse to stop. It could even awaken painful memories of being a victim of child sexual abuse yourself.

Whatever you decide, it will help if you can give the child some control over the actions you take. You could share your worry with someone who knows the family. Contact the NSPCC Child Protection Helpline, the Royal Scottish Society for the Prevention of Cruelty to Children or the Irish Society for the Prevention of Cruelty to Children (see pages 207–9). Or you can contact your local social services department or the police. Seek their advice. It is preferable that you identify yourself and give details but you *can* speak to these organisations, the police and social services anonymously.

Anyone made aware that a child is being abused has a duty to pass the information on to social services and/or the police. This includes schools, doctors, health visitors, mid-wives and support organisations. All relevant professionals or agencies are required to assist social services in their enquiries. Any actions taken will be aimed at the best interests of the child.

Tabitha

I was abused from the age of two until I was seventeen by my father. I wasn't going to say anything but I was living next door to my dad and his new partner, who has a child by him, and I became aware that their son was showing signs of abuse. Seeing that little boy...I couldn't stand the guilt. I went to the police and, from my medical records and evidence given by my mum, there was enough evidence to prosecute my dad. My dad employed a private investigator to provide evidence that I was a promiscuous teenager in an attempt to strengthen his case. When we went to court five years ago I collapsed at one point while I was giving evidence. The judge ordered a stay of the indictment, which meant that although my dad wasn't being acquitted, he wasn't being convicted either.

The Crown Prosecution Service could not believe it. They issued a statement saying, We were as confident as ever we could be as to the prospects of a conviction. I was awarded compensation but I haven't had a relationship with a man since I was seventeen – I'm in my thirties now. I know logically that not all men are the same but I can't help feeling it. I no longer feel I'm losing out in that respect any more. But as for the rest of my life...what my dad did to me and that court case – it's wrecked my life.

If you are under sixteen and experiencing sexual abuse, what should you do?

Try to tell someone you trust about it. If that person does not believe you, keep telling them or other people you trust until someone does believe you. Call ChildLine or the NSPCC Helpline (see pages 207–208).

What happens when you or a child reports child abuse?

The police and social services have to have a disclosure from the child him- or herself in order to investigate, which they will do jointly.

The social services can apply to the courts for a Child Assessment Order, which a magistrate may grant. The order will state the kind of examination and/or tests that may be carried out. It will also state who will carry out the examination and where it will take place.

A social worker will record details of injuries or abuse and will want to know how the injuries happened. The investigation will include all the children in the family. In most cases a doctor will also examine the child. It may be possible to identify the abuser from this evidence. The child is allowed to have a trusted adult with them during the medical examination. A parent or carer, or even an older child, could request the doctor use an appropriate-sized speculum for the child's age and sexual maturity.

If the child is accompanied by a parent or carer who is not aware the child is sexually active, then, after consent has been given by them or by the child for the examination, the child can ask that they leave the room. The child can then answer the doctor's questions freely.

Sometimes a course of antibiotics is offered, which covers all sexually transmitted infections (STIs). 'I do this for young clients who may not return for their follow-up at the genito-urinary clinic,' says Dr Ruhi Jawad at The Haven, a sexual-assault referral centre (SARC) in London. (For further details on sexual-offences examinations, please refer to Chapter 8.)

The social worker will meet the people who have been involved in the investigation for a conference. The parents also usually attend. The conference takes place within two weeks of the referral. They will consider the results of the investigation, then they will discuss what action needs to be taken to make sure the child can live safely in the future.

The social services will have to decide if the child is in immediate danger or harm. They have a duty to protect the child and if the only way is by removing the child from the family home they will do so. However, the law does recommend that children should remain at home whenever possible and the person suspected of carrying out the abuse should leave the family home, at least while the investigation is being carried out. The social services can apply to the courts for an Emergency Protection Order. A magistrate may grant this order when a parent refuses to allow their child to be taken to a safe place.

Will the child have to go to court?

The child will be asked to give a video statement. Social workers and police are allowed to record only one video statement from a child. Only in exceptional circumstances, for example if new evidence emerges, can the police record a second statement and they must obtain permission from the CPS. One social worker explained that less than two hours after one child she knew had given her video statement, the perpetrator was arrested. The video statement will be used as the main evidence if the case reaches court.

In cases of sexual violence, children under the age of seventeen may not have to go into the courtroom at all. Instead, their evidence may be video-recorded and cross-examination may be done by means of a closed-circuit television (CCTV) link.

During the cross-examination the child may be accompanied by a supportive adult. Alternatively, the child may sit in court for the cross-examination but speak from behind a screen, provided the judge grants the request. A child may see the video recording of their first interview before they are cross-examined, to remind them of what they said.

The local police or the NSPCC can provide a Child Witness Pack. It aims to make giving evidence in child-abuse cases less of a traumatic experience for children and their families.

The Child Protection Register

This is a list of the names of children who social services know have suffered child abuse. It may be sexual, physical and/or neglect. It will also list the names of children who are believed to be at risk of abuse. The register is kept by social services and is strictly confidential to them and to health service workers. A social worker will be responsible for watching over the child. He or she will keep in touch with the child's doctor and teachers and will work with the parents to give the child the help they need.

Child sexual abuse in Northern Ireland

Adult survivors of child sexual abuse in Northern Ireland disclose the use of, or threat of, weapons more often than their UK counterparts. Eileen Calder of the Rape Crisis and Sexual Abuse Centre in Northern Ireland describes some of the most extreme of these cases: 'One eight-year-old girl had an illegal gun put in her mouth by her abusing father, another was taken into a field at a farm outside a small country town and watched her pet dog being shot dead with the threat that the same would happen to her or her mother if she did not comply to his demands. She was ten years old at the time.' And while their abuse as children may have had no specific connection with paramilitaries or the political situation, adult survivors do describe experiences that can generally be linked to the

Troubles. 'Anne was sexually abused as a child aged four to seventeen,' says Eileen. 'The daily catalogue of abuse she suffered included full intercourse and anal rape. She had a gun put in her mouth and was threatened with death when she was fifteen years old. Her crime against the community was bringing a Catholic friend into the area.'

Lydia

I was drug-raped by a man a year ago, when I was fifteen. He was part of a big group of people I was with and I knew him through a friend. He threatened that if I said anything, he'd kill me. The next day a friend could see something was wrong and asked me to talk to her. Eventually she persuaded me and she admitted the same man had done it to her – but she wasn't interested in telling anyone about it. Another friend convinced me to tell a teacher at school and she suggested I tell my parents. I went to my GP, who sent me to a sexual-assault referral centre. A couple of weeks had passed by then so it was too late for an exam, but they did a pregnancy test, checked for bruising and tested for STIs. They also sorted out a counsellor for me. But I couldn't get the thought out of my head, Did I say yes? Did I say yes? I also felt guilty because I'd been drinking that night. It was hard for me to sleep and when I did I dreamt about it. The police took him in for questioning and he denied it all. My friend who said he'd done it to her wouldn't back me up and other people called me a liar, said I was just trying to get attention. I self-harmed and felt terrified that he'd track me down and do something. For ages I couldn't bear even to talk to boys. Eventually I started seeing someone and it's taken me ages to trust him, even to allow myself to be alone with him. I've now talked to other survivors and that's really helped. I realised this man took advantage of me. It wasn't my fault. I'm gutted he got away with it in terms of a conviction. I wish I'd gone to the police earlier. But I'm very pleased I reported it. It might make him feel he can't do it again.

3

Stranger Rape

What we imagine to be a typical stranger rape is what most of us will instantly associate with the crime. And when we fear rape, it is this scenario that forms the basis of our fears.

Most stranger rapes probably fit our stereotype. A man we have never met leaps out at night, drags us somewhere we cannot be seen and threatens to use, or uses, violence before or while raping us.

These elements feature strongly in what has been called the 'real rape' model. It is called this because it is how most of us see rape, what we consider to be real rape. Studies have shown that survivors often cope better if their rape fits this model. They are less likely to blame themselves and therefore may feel less guilt than survivors of other forms of rape. This means they might feel more inclined to talk to people about what's happened, to seek help and to report to the police.

Research has also shown that a survivor of stranger rape might have an easier time with the police than survivors of other types of rape. Consequently her case is more likely to advance through the criminal justice system and for a rape conviction to be secured in court.

One study showed that stranger-rape survivors blamed themselves less for the rape, saw themselves in a more positive light and felt closer to recovery six months after the rape than women raped by an acquaintance.

What is stranger rape and who are its victims?

There is no one definition of stranger rape used by police forces across the country. The Metropolitan Police define 'Stranger 1' as rape where the offender has had no prior contact with the victim, or where the offender's knowledge of the victim is gained by close observation, for example by stalking her.

According to research by the Women's National Commission, detailed in their 'Growing Up Female in the UK' report, the highest proportion of stranger rapes occur of women under the age of 21 years. Older women are more likely to experience rape by a partner.

Statistics also show that stranger rape itself is the least likely form of rape that women in general might experience. It constitutes 8 per cent of all reported rapes; whereas rape by a partner has occurred in 45 per cent of cases reported. This is not to say that stranger rape is somehow less important. The proportion of women to whom it happens may be small, but this still translates to many thousands of women who are victims of this crime.

Personal safety

Many women believe that if they follow personal-safety measures, rape cannot happen to them. They also often believe that if it ever did, they would physically resist a rape. Yet when it comes to it the woman might freeze with fear. And even if she didn't, should she fight back anyway? After all, no one can predict which rapist is capable of extreme physical violence or even murder.

'We do not generally give advice on personal safety,' says Lynne Harne, 'because the overwhelming danger to women in relation to sexual violence is not from strangers but from men they know – whether they are dates, friends or partners. So the Rape Crisis Federation and its member groups have a policy not to give advice which is largely useless. In any situation women should not be made to feel responsible for being raped. The responsibility lies with those men who perpetrate it.'

The Suzy Lamplugh Trust was launched in December 1986 following the abduction and murder of Suzy Lamplugh, daughter of the Trust's founder, Diana. The aim of the Trust is to enable people to prevent problems or to deal with, defuse or avoid a confrontation rather than engage in a last-minute defence.

Diana Lamplugh says that personal-safety precautions can stop you living your life afraid of what might happen next. 'It's not about people curtailing your freedom, telling you what to do. It just gives you ideas and you decide whether you want to use them. And if you use them so much they become automatic then that enables you to have more confidence.'

'If you have greater confidence, research has shown you are less likely to become a victim than someone who is confused, lost and worried,' adds Ann Elledge, also of the Trust. 'Even if you're in a situation where things have already started to go wrong, having already thought ahead and asked, "What if?" and made plans means you will perhaps be able to begin to take action before something develops beyond your control. It could help you avoid being numbed by the trauma.'

But it's important to stress that if you have failed to take precautions, or you've taken every one you can think of and you are raped or you feel unable to take action while you are being raped, you have not failed. The rape was not your fault. Rape is never the fault of the survivor. All the blame lies with the rapist.

Should I fight back?

The law and self-defence
NOTE: The following information does not constitute legal advice, nor does it condone the use of force other than for self-defence, purposes.

Under the Criminal Act 1967, you may use reasonable force to defend yourself against an unlawful attack. You're equally entitled to use reasonable force to prevent an unlawful attack upon yourself, your family or your property. However, what constitutes reasonable force and under what circumstances you may use it is open to discussion and may have to be decided by the courts.

The claim of self-defence in court is proved if:

*the defendant genuinely believed they were being attacked or were in imminent danger of attack

* the response was proportionate to the perceived threat

If no threat actually existed but you made a genuine mistake about the existence of a threat, you are entitled to rely on self-defence as your defence.

You do not need to wait until you are hit to use force in your defence. The court of appeal has ruled that '... a defendant is entitled to use self-defence by striking their assailant before they are struck; and in exceptional circumstances, arm them-selves against an expected imminent attack.'

Although your actions should match the level of threat you feel you're under, you don't have to retreat or show unwilling-ness to fight. If the attack is a murderous one, then the defendant would be entitled to use extreme violence.

What can I carry legally?

Personal-attack alarms
Do not rely on these. We tend to ignore most alarms we hear so they are not supposed to bring people running. Carry it in your hand with the safety catch taken off and your finger ready. If you need it, you put it close to your attacker's ear and the sound waves make the ear drum reverberate. They are meant to give out a sound that is as loud as possible without causing permanent damage to hearing. The idea is that it will stun the attacker and give you time to get away.

Weapons

You cannot by law carry anything that could be described as an offensive weapon. And if you carry weapons for protection, for example, a knife, you are more likely to be injured if you are attacked, as the attacker may attempt to use it on you. But if you're under attack and reach for the first available object that comes to hand, the use of that object is likely, in law, to be deemed as reasonable. Everyday items such as pens, hairbrushes etc. can be used against an attacker.

Liz Clark started Women's Self Defence (see page 213) to offer consultation and classes in personal safety and self-defence to individuals and groups, after surviving an attempted rape by a stranger:

I had a few days off and had gone for a walk in the park. It was about 2 p.m., I was wearing a long skirt and a mac and had been sitting on a bench to eat a sandwich when I decided to wander off to look at a nearby stream. But as I stood on a bridge looking at the water a man came and stood next to me. He asked for the time but he made me feel uneasy so I told him quickly and walked away. Unfortunately the direction I took led me into an area with more tree cover. Then I turned and saw he was walking behind me. He was about six foot tall and well built and suddenly he lunged at me and pushed me over. He pinned me down and for a few seconds I was paralysed with fear. I couldn't shout, scream or move. I just knew he was going to rape me. Then he slammed my head against the ground and anger overcame my shock. I began to kick, scratch and fight back. I screamed and screamed and he was yelling at me, Shut up, shut up, saying he'd kill me, telling me he had a knife. His fingers were inside me and he was fumbling for his flies. My whole life flashed in front of me. I thought of my mum, I thought about AIDS. He started to undo his trousers and I was pleading with him not to do it. His whole weight pressed down on me.

But then this survival instinct took over and I decided to let him think I was complying. He believed me and released one of my hands to undo his flies – and that's when I grabbed the back of his head, wrenched my other arm free and poked my fingers into his eyes. I was yanking his head back thinking, What if his eyes pop out? If I see blood I'll pass out and then what? But I wouldn't let go. And still he was trying to rape me. But finally it seemed to dawn on him that I wasn't giving up and he let go. We both stood up and still his fingers were in me so I started whacking him with my bag. And finally he ran off. The whole thing can't have lasted more than five minutes but it felt like five hours. I grabbed my bag and told a woman walking past what had happened. But she said someone had already gone to get the police. There was an investigation but my attacker was never caught.

Straight afterwards I was desperate for him to be caught. I was in the police car driving round the streets wanting to see him again, looking for this guy with scratches on his face. But it was the adrenalin, that's what made me brave. Because a few days later it hit me like a ton of bricks. I'd been bubbly and happy-go-lucky but now I was fearful of everything and I was confrontational with every new bloke I met; to me every one was a potential attacker. I was nineteen when that guy tried to rape me and those feelings of fear and aggression went on for nine years until finally I decided I wouldn't let it ruin my life any more.

I felt inspired to set up my classes. Now I've spoken to hundreds of victims and nine times out of ten the situation arose because they decided to take a risk or they weren't as aware as they should have been of their surroundings. I tell women that if you are attacked you have to try to read your situation as quickly as possible and act accordingly. But fear and adrenalin can make you act or it can make you freeze. Luckily, I only froze for a moment and my gap was him releasing my hands. I thought I'd never trust someone again but I had a couple of relationships and now I'm married with a child.

Women must realise that they can do something positive about their personal safety, whether they have been a victim of crime or not. Women need to and should understand that they do not have to learn the hard way, like I did. If I can stop one other woman from going through what I went through then I'd feel it has all been worth it.'

What if I'm attacked?

Do enough to get away. Don't stand and fight, says Liz Clark. 'You do not want a physical confrontation unless you absolutely cannot avoid it.' But if you can't avoid it, she says, or you cannot run, then aim to fight dirty. 'Pull hair, bite, scratch, flail your arms and kick out. If you're able to be more directional in what you do, go for the eyes.' Clark suggests an eye strike. 'If you can push a doorbell you can perform an eye strike. But don't just use one finger, use them all. The eyes are one part of the body which can cause something called "pain reaction" – where injury causes us to hold the site of the pain. As well as the eyes, we can get this reaction by hitting the jaw, the nose, the throat, the groin, the shins and the feet. This may give you the split second you need by encouraging your attacker to release his grasp. Then you can run.'

What if I freeze?

When we sense danger we get a surge of adrenalin, a chemical found naturally in the body that is preparing us to face an attack or to run. This is known as the 'fight or flight' response.

We freeze not from fear but from confusion. We want to run but are still trying to make sense of what's going on. There's lots of information coming in at once. You can overcome this feeling by screaming, breaking a window, even stepping back. 'When the adrenalin is racing around your body with nowhere to go it can make your legs shake, make you want to cry, even to go to the toilet and to feel paralysed. But by making just one action, however small, you break that cycle. Your adrenalin is telling you to respond by "flight", to run. Believe you can use it,' says Liz Clark.

Edged weapons

To prevent yourself from a serious injury, or worse, from a knife, the golden rule is not to fight someone who has one, stresses Liz Clark. 'Sometimes there will be an opportunity to get away when they have to put the knife down – when they're trying to get you into a car, turn you or put you on the floor, for example. It may only be a split second but it's a chance.'

But if someone grabs you from behind and puts a knife to your neck, there's nothing you can or should do, Clark cautions. 'If you try to grab the knife you could lose your fingers. If you try to grab the attacker's arms it might just tighten his grip. I know of a woman who was in this situation and kicked back at her attacker and managed to get away. But on the whole I would advise against any kind of confrontation with a person with a knife.'

The importance of what you and your body say

A potential attacker works on your being unsure, on your being vulnerable, either by what you say or by your body language. If you are approached you should do your best not to look away quickly or do anything that makes you seem unsure or nervous. 'If someone comes up to you and asks the time, you should keep walking as you check your watch. Have some distance between you when you reply. Appear confident. The same applies if they ask directions. If you're unfamiliar with the area, don't say so. Make something up.

'Also ensure you don't have your arms down by your sides: it's easy to grab round you that way,' says Clark. 'And be aware of your facial expression and your tone of voice. Ask them a question back. This throws them. You can even act crazy, to completely throw them off balance. Stand and scream your head off or run round in circles with your hands in the air. A potential attacker is unlikely to persist if you're making a scene.

'Trust your instincts about people. You don't have to be aggressive. But try not to seem scared because that's when they know they've got you, that you'll comply.'

Thinking ahead

The Suzy Lamplugh Trust advises four clear points to bear in mind, using the word 'plan' as a reminder:

P * Plan ahead. Where am I going? How will I return? If it's a regular journey it's a good idea to vary your route and time of travelling sometimes. Try to organise transport home before you leave. Make a note of the phone numbers of a reputable taxi company and an emergency contact and keep them with your keys, money for the phone, travel card, phone card, your fully charged mobile and money for the journey home. Make sure the money you've set aside for these things is kept separate so you don't accidentally spend it. Try to make sure these things are not in your bag – just in case you need to give it up and/or escape quickly.

L* Let someone know where you are going.

A * Be Aware of the potential problems – and solutions. If you wear heels to work, try to wear trainers instead – you can run more easily in them. But high heels can also be a great weapon, particularly if you're attacked from behind. You can dig them into, or scrape them down, your attacker's shins.

Be alert when you're out and about. Don't stand in the street and let yourself be distracted, for example, by a mobile phone conversation. If you think you're being followed, keep crossing over the road and try to get to a safer area as soon as possible. If you're near shops, restaurants or bars, go in and inform them you think you're being followed and phone the police. Never feel stupid or embarrassed about phoning for help. It is better to be safe than sorry.

When out with friends, stay as a group. Don't split up or leave someone to get home alone. If your plans change, work out a new way to get home safely. If you know you'll be home later than planned, let someone know.

To avoid your drink being spiked – with alcohol or other drugs – try not to leave your glass or bottle unattended. If you feel ill or light-headed, tell someone immediately and ask for a taxi to take you straight home. (Note: there have been reports of barmen and/or door staff being in collusion with other men – letting them know who is drunk and/or drugged and therefore vulnerable. So be careful whom you go to for help.)

N * Never be over-confident. Be alert. Trust your instincts. If you feel your safety is being threatened, move away from the situation, to a public place, as soon as possible. Make as much noise as you can. Your voice can be a good defence. Remember that feeling ill or light-headed – for example through drugs or alcohol – is bound to affect your behaviour and your responses.

Parking your car and using public transport

Make sure you park your car during the day where you will be happy to return to it at night, if that's what you'll need to do. And park it facing in the direction you will be going. You don't want to be negotiating three-point turns or tight reversing if you're in a dangerous situation. Avoid poorly lit car parks and, whenever possible, choose a car park with CCTV or one that's manned and park as close as you can to the attendant.

Make sure your car's interior light is working. Shut all windows and the sunroof and lock doors. Note exactly where you've parked your car. When returning to your car have keys ready to get in quickly. Before you get in, have a quick glance into the back seat. Lock doors immediately and drive off quickly.

If you're taking an overground or underground train, be wary of deserted platforms or footpaths that are screened by fences or vegetation.

Taxis

According to Metropolitan Police Service statistics, between 1 April 2000 and 31 March 2002, 3 per cent of all rapes and sexual assaults reported were committed by male minicab drivers. This translates to 45 rapes and over 200 sexual assaults over that period in London alone. The majority were committed at night.

As mentioned in the 'thinking ahead' section, make a note of the telephone number of a trustworthy taxi company and keep money aside for the journey home. Try to share a cab with a friend. If you've not booked a taxi, use black cabs or registered taxis (hackney carriages). These are licensed by the police or local authority and have identity numbers.

Some people represent themselves falsely as minicab drivers with roof aerials and false handsets. They wait at night in busy nightspots and might call out, 'Anyone ordered a cab?' Or offer you a good fare. On a busy night when there is a shortage of transport this could be tempting. But you should not be tempted. You must not think, It won't ever happen to me.

If you are calling a cab from a public place, ask for the driver's name and the make and colour of the car. Try not to let people overhear your name and address. Anyone could pretend to be your cab. Wait inside the venue or with the door supervisors. When he arrives, check the driver's name and the company and what name he is expecting to collect. Since October 2001, it has been illegal to operate as a minicab firm in London without a licence from the Public Carriage Office. There are now 2,100 licensed operators across the capital but, at the time of writing, Transport for London is about to begin the process of licensing all of London's 40,000-plus minicab drivers.

Drivers will be required to provide a signed health certificate and will undergo a full criminal-record check. If cleared, they will be given an ID card with photo, which they will be required to wear.

Some nightclubs are also starting to run their own minicab firms and police are considering the introduction of safety zones where women can go and get cabs safely.

To check if a firm in London is licensed, ask to see its certificate at its offices or contact Transport for London. For information on this and on women-only cab firms in the capital, see Help at the end of this book.

Try not to travel alone. You could also stay at a friend's house or vice versa. If you can't do this then tell friends you will call them soon to check they're home. Make sure the driver hears you say this. If you're leaving friends to take a cab alone, make sure they take down the details of the cab, or call someone on your mobile as you get in to let them know you're on your way and to give them the taxi details (you can even leave this on your answer machine if you live alone). Again, make sure the driver is aware that your friends and you are doing this.

Always sit at the back of the taxi. If something happens, it's easier to attack from behind. If you chat to the driver, don't give him any personal details.

If you feel at all threatened, ask the driver firmly to stop – if possible in a busy place – and get out. If he refuses to stop and you truly believe you are in danger, try to alert other drivers by waving out of the window. Scream, make it obvious you're in danger.

Weigh up the situation. Is the driver aggressive? Does he have a knife? Are you wearing a seatbelt? Is he driving very fast? Depending on the circumstances, you could try to get out at a junction or at traffic lights. If the doors are unlocked you could grab his ears and turn them, as if you were squeezing a wet rag, to break his concentration and enable you to escape.

If the journey goes without a hitch, still make sure you have your fare ready and your keys in your hand. Ask the driver to wait in his taxi until you get safely inside. If you live alone, make sure you've left a light on at home before you leave so it doesn't look as if you're going home to an empty house.

Kelly

I had been at my work Christmas party and then gone on to a bar with a group of colleagues before deciding it was time to head for home. I climbed into one of several minicabs outside the bar and must have fallen asleep but I woke with a start to find the driver had his hand on my knee as we waited at some lights. I pushed it away and told him to get lost. Then I dozed off again. When I woke the next time the driver was on top of me. All at once I was confused, panicked and realised he was raping me. When he climbed off I scrambled out of the car. As he drove away I realised we were in the car park of a library only a couple of minutes from my house.

Suddenly what had happened hit me. I felt disgusting and blamed myself. Why had I drunk so much? When I got in I was crying uncontrollably. I was insisting I needed a shower, telling my flatmates I felt horrible. I didn't tell them what had happened but they worked it out. They wouldn't let me shower and took me to the police station. From there a specially trained officer was assigned to me and took me for an examination. Afterwards I had a bath and was given some fresh clothing. Then the officer took me home. The next day my assigned officer took my statement. I got very upset, having to relive it all, but he was very understanding. After that he kept in touch, updating me. Then, after a few weeks, he called to say they'd found a match on DNA – the driver had a criminal record and they'd brought him in for questioning. The police asked if I wanted to press charges and two things convinced me I would. One was that the man claimed I had consented; the other was that he'd described me as blonde. I'm not blonde and it made me wonder, How many other times has this man done this and how many more times will he do it?

I went to court twelve months after I was raped. In the run-up I was very nervous. But my assigned officer and the investigating officer encouraged me and supported me. And they took me to the courtroom in advance so I knew what to expect. On the day they advised me to keep my answers short and to simply tell the truth. The driver's defence said I'd taken one of his business cards and said I'd call him the next day. He claimed I'd used language to encourage him to have sex with me that I've never used with anyone in an intimate moment. I was on the stand for about an hour and a half but I was so angry that this man had said all these things that that gave me the strength to carry on and defend myself. Afterwards the officers told me how well I'd done. But I just wanted to go home. The next day the jury came back with a unanimous verdict. The investigating officer called to tell me he'd been found guilty and they'd sentenced him to eight years. I was so happy.

I haven't had a relationship since all this happened and it's only now I even feel able to consider counselling. But I wonder what state I'd be in if I hadn't had the support I've had from my friends and the police. I can't put into words my gratitude for all my assigned officer and the investigating officer did for me. They gave me their mobile numbers, kept in touch so I always felt they cared about me . . . they kept me going for that entire year. Without them that man might still be free.

Danger areas

Find out about the high-risk places in your area from Neighbour-hood Watch groups and the police. If you feel somewhere could be safer, contact your local council. Under Section 17 of the Crime and Disorder Act, local authorities are obliged to do all they reasonably can to prevent crime and disorder.

Don't take short cuts. Walk the long way round or get a licensed taxi. And try to avoid being alone in, or move quickly away from:

* The streets near pubs and clubs at closing time. According to the 2000 British Crime Survey, victims judged that 'their' offenders were under the influence of alcohol in 40 per cent of incidents of violence. This was most likely for stranger violence. Overall offenders were judged to be under the influence of drugs in 18 per cent of incidents.

* Bright, high, orange streetlights. We feel safe in areas with street lighting but recent research has shown that attackers are more likely to succeed near these lights because they throw long shadows where they can hide and they only show people in silhouette, so it's hard to make out who's walking towards you. Other danger points are where street lighting thins out on side roads. It takes time for your eyes to adjust and this may make you vulnerable.

* Litter and graffiti. This can be a sign that residents don't keep close watch over the area. Criminals could feel it's less likely that someone will step in if an offence is being committed.

* Built-up areas. Don't be lulled into a false sense of security simply because there are lots of houses and/or flats around. The design of the development might provide opportunities for attack.

* Footpaths, alleys and doorways. The only way of escaping when you're in an alley is forwards or back the way you came,

not necessarily easy if one or more people are blocking your path. Walk on the outside of the pavement to make you less vulnerable to being dragged into alleys and doorways. Also, walk on the right side of the road, facing oncoming traffic to avoid kerb crawlers.

*Parks and waste or recreation ground. Try to steer clear of tree- or bush-lined paths. They provide opportunities to pull you in.

Emma

I was walking home from work at about 5 p.m. It was December so it was quite dark. I was cutting through a churchyard but it was in the middle of the city and used by lots of people as a regular shortcut. As I went in that day, though, I had an inexplicable feeling of uneasiness. There were quite a few people around but suddenly they all seemed to disappear – except for a man leaning against the church wall holding a red bag. I felt awkward but tried not to attract his attention by just continuing towards the path which led to the top of the street where I lived. But he walked towards me. I was terrified. He grabbed me by the arms and demanded, 'Give us a kiss.'

I tried to think quickly and told him my boyfriend was waiting at the other end. I just wanted to get away. I tried to cut to the other path, to put some distance between us. But he wouldn't let me pass. So I decided to try another tactic. We sat on a bench behind us and I offered to get him some help. He was very agitated and I thought that if I talked to him and could pacify him he might let me go. But after we'd been talking for about ten minutes he started saying I was his girlfriend. I realised this was doing no good and got up to leave. But he grabbed hold of me again. He asked if I had any money, so I emptied my purse and gave him the £1.20 in there. But that made him angry. He said I must have more money in my bag. He went for my handbag and we struggled. The thought went through my head, It's just a bag, let him take it. But before I could let go he punched me in the head. Then he grabbed my bag – but he didn't leave. It crossed my mind what might happen next. I was so scared. I tried to leave again but he took hold of my arms, spun me and pushed me into some bushes. I cried and begged him not to hurt me. But he wouldn't listen. He forced himself on top of me and kept shouting at me to get my underwear off. I thought, If I give in he'll let me go. So I did. It was awful. All the way through the attack I tried to detach myself from what was happening. He was sniffing nail varnish from the red bag and was high on the fumes. He stank.

The next twenty-five minutes seemed to last a lifetime. I remember looking up at a tree and thinking, Is this the last thing I'll ever see? The thought of dying at nineteen... I kept asking questions, anything to distract myself from what was going on. He disgusted me. Then when it was over he changed. He asked if I had my bag, as if nothing had happened. I was numb. What was he thinking? He had just raped me! He then began looking for something – the bottle of nail varnish from which he'd been sniffing. I gathered together my things and picked up my torn knickers. I was thinking about evidence... I must have been on auto-pilot. He asked me to help him find his nail varnish so I said, 'I'll take you into town to buy you some.' I just wanted to get back into a public place so I could run. But just then someone came into the churchyard. This was my chance to escape. I ran as fast as I could and reached the top of my street. I was so out of breath. And it was at that moment that the sheer enormity of it all hit me. I started to cry uncontrollably. My whole body shook and my face felt as if it was going to curl up. I'd never cried like that.

Then a group of people passed. We were near a school and they looked as if they'd just come out of a meeting. One of the women noticed I was upset and I told her what had happened. Then we hugged. I didn't know her but I suddenly felt safe. She and a man from the group took me home in their car. I got a change of clothes and my lodger drove me to the hospital. He kept commenting on how calm I was. But I was just so happy to be alive. I had minor injuries but did not feel any pain until a few days later. Then I went to the police station. By the time I got there they already had my attacker in custody. After he'd raped me, he'd tried to snatch a woman's handbag – obviously to find money for his habit – and he got caught. During the rape he'd made me give him a love bite and I did it really hard so that it would be noticeable, and perhaps would be useful to identify him, if I got away. In retrospect I can't believe I had the presence of mind to do that – and to pick up my underwear.

He ended up getting ten years for robbery and rape. He pleaded guilty so I never got to attend the initial hearing. However, I felt I needed to see his face, to help me cope with what had happened. I later wrote to him in prison and asked how he felt about what he'd done. His reply made it obvious that he had little insight into the seriousness of his crime. He wrote back via the police. His letter was covered in little drawings, as if a child had written it. He wrote, 'I was so shocked to hear that I got ten years. If I could turn back the clock I would . . . I hope we can still be friends . . . '

Six months later my attacker appealed against his sentence. Now was my chance to face him. I went to the court of appeal in London on my own. I felt it was something I had to do. During the hearing I cried silently to myself. He looked so grey and sad standing in the dock. I just felt sorry for him. It was difficult but it did help to put things into perspective. In the following months I did a lot of thinking. That was five years ago. I am now married and have recently graduated from university. I think of the attack every day but can talk openly about it. I think this is because my way of coping with the attack was by facing all the fears I had associated with it. I forced myself to go out on my own and to carry on with all the normal things that people do. I was determined to deal with what had happened and to experience all the emotions, some *of which had become difficult since the rape – love, intimacy, close friendship and, more importantly, loving myself. I have always known that this could have happened to anyone, that I hadn't caused this man to rape me. I didn't lead him on in some strange way. If you've survived rape you have to know that to be able to move on in life. You must put the blame and guilt to one side. That's for the rapist to deal with, not you.*

'You need to weigh up situations and ask yourself, Will I be, or am I comfortable, taking risks here?' says Ann Elledge of the Suzy Lamplugh Trust. 'If you say, I don't want my life to be curtailed in any way, then you are also saying you are taking on board the risks.

'You don't have to feel restricted by looking after your personal safety. Instead, you should feel empowered that you can make decisions and develop skills which can become so automatic and instinctive you can live life to the full.'

Rape can happen anywhere and at any time. So you should be aware at all times and pay attention to your intuition. Use your common sense and never put yourself in a position you don't have to be in.

If you find yourself in a potential rape situation, you need to weigh up the odds. Ask yourself, Is there any chance here, any opportunity for me, are the dangers so great that my best option is to do nothing?

'Keep talking, stalling, walking, anything to give you vital seconds,' says Liz Clarke. 'But if you are attacked and you do nothing, remind yourself you were scared, perhaps there was nothing you could have done – maybe not resisting or playing dead saved you from serious injury or from actually losing your life. You might have felt there were no choices, that your only option was to let it happen, but that was a choice in itself and one that *you* made – not your attacker. Reminding yourself of this, believing it, can help you in recovery. However you choose to get through rape you are a survivor.'

4

Acquaintance Rape

When someone you know rapes you, it shatters a situation in which you had felt safe, it can make you question your own judgement and can overwhelm you with feelings of guilt that you have caused this normally safe situation, and the person in it, to change.

If you've flirted with this man, even indulged in some foreplay with him, and ended up being forced to have penetrative sex, the self-blame can be even more acute.

In a 2001 *Cosmopolitan* sex-crimes survey, as many as two out of three women who had been victims of sex crime knew their offender. Statistics taken from calls to Rape Crisis Federation groups in 2001 showed that 73 per cent of women and girls were assaulted by a man who was known to them. And according to British Crime Survey 2000 results, 92 per cent of women and girls were sexually assaulted by a man who was known to them.

What is acquaintance or date rape?

What is sometimes referred to as 'acquaintance' or 'date' rape is called 'Stranger 2' by the Metropolitan Police (but not other forces). They define it as 'where the knowledge of the victim is limited to the period immediately before the assault or where the victim and suspect were briefly known to one another, for example, they had met at a party, club or bar or had a client/prostitute relationship.'

According to the Home Office, almost half of acquaintance rapes involved somebody the victim had known for less than 24 hours. And the British Crime Survey 2000 says 16 per cent of rapes reported to them were by people the victim had 'met casually for the first time'.

However, 'intimate rape' – sometimes referred to as 'relationship' or 'domestic' rape – is a misleading term. Because as well as referring to rape where the offender was having a relationship, or had had a previous relationship, with the victim (11 per cent of rapes coming to the attention of the British Crime Survey), 'intimates' can also refer to friends, members of your family, neighbours or colleagues. These are people in your life whom you may well describe as acquaintances. The survey reported that 10 per cent of rapes were in this category.

But surely it's not as traumatic as being raped by a stranger?

There was at one time serious discussion about creating a lesser offence of acquaintance rape but this has been firmly rejected. The 2000 Home Office report 'Setting the Boundaries' said, 'The crime of rape is so serious that it needs to be considered in its totality rather than being constrained by any relationship between the parties ... there is neither justification nor robust grounds for grading rape into lesser or more serious offences.'

Liz Kelly's review for the CPS inspectorate in 2002 points out that research on rape in marriage, as well as other studies that compare the effects of rape by strangers and acquaintances, 'all point to there being no less trauma or injury where the rapist is known'. In fact, she continues, 'in terms of betrayal of trust and disruption to self-image, assaults by known assailants have greater impacts.'

Analysis of the effects on survivors of acquaintance rape has shown it can be dramatic and long-lasting. Many change their lifestyle, move house through fear that the rapist might return, have time off or give up work, break up their relationships and require long-term medication and counselling. It also makes them more fearful of men generally – if I can't trust the men I know, who can I trust?

Reporting to the police and going to court

Despite the fact that research shows it is this type of rape that is most common, rapes by a man known to the victim are less likely to be reported and less likely to result in successful prosecution than those by unknown assailants.

Because acquaintance rape most often happens in a domestic setting, usually his place or yours, with no witnesses, then it is your word against the rapist's. This, combined with the self-blame and battering to self-confidence you may well be experiencing, could make you reluctant to face the police. Perhaps you fear they could add to that blame. And you might be wary that if your case reaches court you will be humiliated all over again on the witness stand.

Research has shown that in terms of securing convictions, there are difficulties because the fact that the woman knows her attacker – however briefly – often diverts attention from the crime. And while it is perhaps not as hard as in cases of rape by partners or husbands, proving lack of consent can be very problematic.

The fact that women feel they cannot predict how the police will react to them and that they may end up being exposed to the widely reported shortcomings of the judicial system makes it understandable that they might feel reluctant about reporting the rape. And this is, of course, their choice. But not reporting leaves those rapists free to carry on with their behaviour and possibly without conviction. One piece of US research carried out by Lisak and Miller in the late 1990s suggests that date rapists often rape over and over again. Of the sample group, 63 per cent reported committing multiple rapes, averaging almost six rapes each.

According to the 1998 study 'Young People's Attitudes Towards Violence, Sex and Relationships', which talked to men between the ages of 14 and 21, there were many circumstances in which they thought it might be acceptable for a man to rape a woman. One in ten thought there was nothing wrong in a man forcing a woman to have sex if he was 'so turned on he can't stop'. Other circumstances in which they thought it might be acceptable included if 'he's spent a lot of money on her' or if 'she'd slept with loads of men'. Also if 'nobody would find out'.

Susan Van Scoyoc is a chartered counselling psychologist and is clinical director of The Women's Practice, a women's counselling service, with branches in Essex and Harley Street in London. She has also often been an expert witness in rape trials, drawing up psychological reports on rapists and rape victims. She says, 'In so-called date rape it is about the rapist believing that he has done nothing out of the ordinary – nothing wrong – and that he can say hello the next time you meet and all is well.'

Claire

I was asked by a friend if her brother could stay at my flat. I'd met him before and had got on well with him. I picked him up from the station and on the way home he talked about how his wife had died a few weeks earlier and how he'd been abused as a child. When we got back I said he could have my bed and popped in to check if he needed anything. He asked me, 'Will you hold me?' I saw this only in the context of what he'd been telling me earlier and climbed on the bed. But he grabbed my wrists and tried to kiss me. I struggled and said 'No' over and over again but he held me down. Over the next four hours he raped me vaginally and anally four times. Then he left without saying a word.

I had no intention of going to the police. I'd been stranger-raped ten years earlier and was treated appallingly on the night it happened, then never contacted again. But ten days after this second attack, I started to get a nasty discharge and went to my local GU clinic. I told them what had happened and they told me about The Haven, a sexual-assault referral centre near where I live. I decided to go and the forensic nurse there took a statement from me while I drank coffee and had a cigarette. I was given tests for STIs and a pregnancy test and was given antibiotics. I agreed that the information I'd given could be passed to the police. Then two days later I called The Haven and was told the police were keen to talk to me. They already had something on my friend's brother but couldn't tell me what in case it affected any evidence I gave.

I met two officers from Project Sapphire, police in London who specialise in rape investigation. One was a chaperone officer assigned to me. He was wonderful. They asked if I'd like to take things further and I decided I would. I saw my chaperone four times for my police statement to be taken – three of them at my home. He wore plain clothes so there was no explaining to do to neighbours. As well as the forensics from my examination, the police also took samples from my home. I'd washed the sheets but apparently evidence can still be picked up. My infection cleared up and I've being seeing a counsellor. Jo, the forensic nurse, calls me and says I can come in for a coffee and a chat any time. Meanwhile, I'm waiting to hear back from the police when the forensics are returned from the lab. I'm no longer in touch with my friend. She said I shouldn't have reported. But at least now the police have more information on her brother. I have no doubt I did the right thing. The Haven made me feel I was back in control and my chaperone never put any pressure on me. I cannot thank the Sapphire team and The Haven

enough. My experience has been so different to ten years ago.
They listened to me, they took care of me. They've given me a
safe space to sort my life out.

Trying to avoid acquaintance rape, dealing with it and surviving it

Early behaviour in any form of relationship that says this man
is a poor personal-safety choice can include obvious things
like physical abuse. But you should also be aware of emotional
abuse, such as verbal put-downs, isolating you from those
close to you (for example, becoming possessive of your social,
or even close family, life after only a couple of dates) and trying
to make you do things in bed that you're not happy with.

What you can say

Say 'No' to a request, not 'No' to the person. 'I don't want you
to do that,' rather than, 'I don't like you.' Saying 'no' to him as
a person can be like showing a red rag to a bull. If someone
feels inadequate it can feel like rubbing salt into a wound.
When you speak to him, look him in the eye and use a firm,
clear voice.

'It can be difficult but you must not feel you have to be polite
until someone goes away,' says Susan Van Scoyoc. 'Be clear
what you mean. Raise your voice if he is not responding,
especially if you are in company.

'If he's getting too close or touching you and you don't want
him to, tell him to back off. Say, "I want you to stop that now." If
he persists, tell him you've not agreed to have sex with him. If
you can, simply walk away. If you give him any excuse to think
you are interested, you are putting yourself in more danger.'

If things have reached a point where a rape seems
imminent, continuing to say 'No' may not help – you have been
ignored so far. Pleading and crying may be equally useless.

Your attacker may think:

* you want it but just don't want to seem easy

* you're shy, scared or inexperienced

* this is not rape

So, say as firmly and as often as you can:

* 'This is rape. This is not consensual sex. This is not love. Rape is a crime and if you carry on I will report you to the police and I will prosecute you.'

* 'I will tell your family and friends.'

But, if this makes him more aggressive, then backtrack and:

* try to calm him down

*attempt to get him to see you as identifiable, like his mother or sister, not as an object. Talk about yourself. Say, 'Would you want someone to do this to your sister?'

But remember, because there is no one type of man who rapes, you can never predict how he will react to the things you say. You may be panicking or very frightened but try to be as aware of his responses as you can. If you feel your comments might be escalating the situation, change tack or say nothing more.

What you can do

Research has shown that we are less likely to actively resist people we know than those who are strangers. But US research on resistance strategies by Professor Sarah Ullman from the University of Illinois has also shown that in cases of date rape, active resistance can help and does not usually escalate violence. 'A woman's level of physical injury is mainly determined by the offender's use of violence and initial blows struck, not because she fought back,' says Professor Ullman.

'By not resisting rape,' she stresses, 'women may be putting themselves at greater risk.'

Diana Lamplugh suggests that if you find saying 'No', reasoning or even struggling does no good then you could pretend you're about to be sick. 'Retch loudly and, if you're lucky, he'll recoil long enough for you to get away.' She also suggests that, if you can reach it, it may be worth using a personal alarm. 'If you spot or make any opportunity to escape you should use it, even if it means leaving some or all of your clothes behind.'

(See pages 43–6 for tips on using a personal alarm and for more advice on personal safety.)

Using the Internet

* If you make a date on the Net, or respond to a newspaper advertisement, or even if you're just chatting, don't give out personal details – phone number, name, address or a personal description. Even a phone number might lead someone to your address.

* Arrange to meet in a busy public place where you will be able to get away easily.

* Take a friend along to meet your date and then ask her to come back at a pre-arranged time. Also work out a pre-arranged signal with your friend to indicate if you would rather she stay with you.

* Tell someone where you are going, with whom (including name, phone number and address) and when you'll be back.

* Initially, don't go home with your date, don't invite him back to your home or even accept a lift.

* Pay attention to your instincts. If you feel uneasy about someone, there may be a good reason. Don't tell yourself you're being silly. If you feel uncomfortable don't reveal personal details and don't arrange a second date.

Gina

I'd known him since I was a child. He knows my mum well. But I never had much contact with him, or interest in him. He's fourteen years older than me. Recently I'd seen him more often, even stayed over at his place and helped with his children. But then he'd done some things that I found really irritating and we'd argued. He came round to my house shortly afterwards and suggested we should get on because it might upset my family. He mentioned he was going shopping and asked if I'd like to come along. While we were out, he bought me some clothes. Then he asked if I'd like to go back to his place for a drink. It was a Friday night, I was in a good mood after getting the clothes and I said 'Yes'. I drank quite a lot and decided to stay the night and sleep it off. I got into one of the children's beds – they weren't around that night – and went out like a light.

But I was woken from a deep sleep soon after. He was on top of me. It took a moment to fully realise what was happening, then I sort of zoned out. It was so weird. I froze, I couldn't move. I just turned my head to the side. He kept saying, 'It's all right, it's all right.' And in my head I was screaming, 'No, it's not, I've known you since I was a little girl.' Twice he said, 'What are you doing?' to himself and that frightened me. It was as if he couldn't help himself. I wondered, If he suddenly feels guilty, what will he do to me next? I knew he had a bad temper. I wondered if he'd murder me. I just wanted to pretend it wasn't happening and wait until he finished. I was crying so much it was soaking my hair. I looked at the clock and finally, after an hour, he stopped.

Fifteen minutes later he was asleep. I was still numb with fear but I knew I had to take this chance to escape. I slid out of the bed, grabbed all my clothes and crept downstairs. But as I reached the front door he came to the top of the stairs. I fumbled with the key and bolted out. It was about 4 a.m. and I was miles from anywhere with no money. I ran and ran until finally I found a supermarket with people working in there. I started banging on the window, crying, telling them what had happened. They got me a taxi and soon I was home. My mum called the police for me and they came and took my clothes and underwear and asked me what had happened. It was hard to talk about it. It seemed like a blur.

Later that day a detective came, then a forensic doctor who conducted an examination. After they'd gone I had a long bath. I was so relieved the police had been so understanding but I was also pleased that part of it was over. Within a day the police had arrested him and searched his house. There's now a court order preventing him coming anywhere near our house, my family or me. The police said it would take about six weeks to get back the forensics, so that's any day now. At first I felt I'd done wrong. I thought, I shouldn't have got so drunk. I felt really angry and was very hostile to everyone. But people helped me gradually to realise that he was the one who'd done wrong. I'm determined not to let him ruin my life. This will make me stronger. I refuse to think every man is a sex attacker like him.

I hope my case goes to court. I'm looking forward to it. Even if he's not convicted I'll know I did all I could. I'd have felt so guilty if I hadn't reported, knowing he could do it to someone else. But he crossed a line and I'll do all I can to make sure he doesn't get away with that.

Rape at work

Aside from the trauma of the rape itself, being raped at work has a specific set of difficulties. You may feel you don't want to report for fear of the repercussions for you professionally and personally or that you cannot simply resign, for the same reasons. You could lose your home or be unable to support dependants. To pursue a report might also adversely affect your career path. If the rape is recorded, how will prospective employers react?

If you tell your employer what's happened and are sacked, you could be facing a legal battle for unfair dismissal. On the other hand, your employer may be sympathetic – yet you may still be suspended, with all the difficulty and trauma that could involve, pending an investigation. And whether nothing at all is done or the matter is resolved to your satisfaction – with or without the police – there could be repercussions for you with colleagues.

'Many women do not say anything when they are sexually harassed, assaulted or raped at work,' says Susan Van Scoyoc. 'Those who do can find it a distressing experience if the company do not take swift action against the other employee. The employer may instead suspend both employees and investigate. The victim may then feel revictimised and not believed. If the employers do not do something then the office tends to split in who they believe. This is damaging to everyone and sometimes very bitchy.'

Should I tell my employer what's happened?

'We know of a woman who is going to a tribunal because she was raped, told her employer and said she would need to take some time off, possibly at short notice and on a number of occasions, to talk to the police. Her employer refused and she resigned,' says Moira Haynes of the Citizens' Advice Bureaux. 'This could be a case of constructive dismissal. It could also be regarded as discriminatory or a breach of mutual trust and confidence, which is a requirement between an employer and employee.

'In our experience employers are often not very supportive in this sort of situation. Of course, you may have a good relationship with your employer and feel you can tell them exactly what's happened. On the other hand, you might be opening yourself up to discriminatory treatment. So it might be better not to disclose what's happened and instead to take time off on grounds of ill health.'

Gill Gridley of Victim Supportline says it depends on the employer but agrees that, generally speaking, rape victims would take time off and only give illness as the reason. 'If you didn't want the employer to know that you had been raped, a GP could write something else on the sick certificate. But it would have to be a recognised medical condition, for example, depression rather than stress. We have heard that sympathetic GPs might write a certificate for something like a virus for a rape victim, if asked. If there were physical injuries, someone might tell their employer that they had been physically assaulted and have a certificate to cover those injuries.

'If someone asked us about this, we would help them to talk through what they wanted to tell their employer, if anything, and help them to decide what they wanted from their GP.'

Hannah

Two days after I began working at the company, Rob joined. I was financial controller and he was a senior sales executive. I had a lot of contact with him and it was my responsibility to make sure all the sales people, including him, toed the line. He disagreed with the standards I set the team and made it very clear by the comments he made.

Six months into our time at the company there was a leaving do for one of our colleagues. It was on a Friday night at a venue across the road from our building. I wasn't drinking much for two reasons – I had a nutritionist appointment the next day and it was also going to be my daughter's birthday party. In fact, people made fun of me because I only had two vodkas then went on to water. I got talking to Rob and we had a nice relaxed chat about our kids and respective spouses. But later in the evening he walked past and asked if I'd ever had an affair. I told him, 'No' and he persisted, 'Have you ever thought about it?' I said, 'Yes' and qualified it by adding that I'd known my husband since we were fifteen and had been married for fourteen years. But I would never do it. Everyone around could hear and agreed: 'There's only one guy for Han,' they said. I found it all a bit weird because not long before we'd been speaking about our families. He just walked off and I realised I should be going. But I worked a lot at weekends and would need to that weekend so I had to get my laptop from the office. A colleague had offered to get it for me a couple of hours earlier when he collected his but I'd said I'd pick it up when I got my cab home. He texted me at 9.30 p.m. saying: 'I've picked up the laptop. Yours is in the cupboard. Be good. See you next week.'

As I was leaving the bar, just after eleven, Rob caught me up. He said he was going for a pee in the office. I wondered why he couldn't use the toilets at the bar but thought he was perhaps being considerate by walking over with me. But when I'd got my laptop I noticed he was sitting in darkness in the boardroom. I stood in the doorway and said, 'Come on, I've got the keys. I need to lock up.' Then he walked up and tried to kiss me. I was taken aback and told him to back off and stop being stupid. But he didn't stop. I took a step away and he said it was too late. That made me feel very frightened.

'What do you mean?' I asked as I continued to walk backwards. But unfortunately the way I'd been standing meant I was backing into the room instead of out of it. Suddenly I had the boardroom table behind me. He had hold of my wrists and wouldn't stop kissing me. I tried to push him off and was really panicking. I started to cry and struggle hard. But he just held tighter, kissing my neck, stroking my hair, saying he'd been wanting to do it all evening. I said we were both married, that it wasn't what I wanted. I was shaking and sobbing and suddenly he stopped. He didn't let go of my wrists but I thought, Thank God he's come to his senses. He told me not to panic, he wasn't going to do anything. He just wanted to hug me, he said. But then he sat on a chair and dragged me on top of him and then to my knees. He began unzipping himself and

said that if I didn't do what he wanted he'd make sure I lost my job. I was paralysed by fear but he held my head and my hair so tightly that I had no choice. I was terrified. I thought, If I can just get this over with I can get home. But he got angry, said I wasn't doing it properly. I was choking and crying and he was threatening me over and over.

Eventually he seemed to decide he was getting nowhere and stood us up before pushing me against the wall. He held my throat and told me to calm down. 'It's only sex,' he said, groping and touching me. He clearly liked me being frightened but was getting very irritated that I wasn't responding to him. He wanted me take his shirt off and I refused. He told me to take my top off and I refused again. It was weird. I thought, If our clothes are on he can't go any further. He pushed me onto the table, really angry now, and leant over me, pinning both my hands over my head with one of his while pulling up my top with the other. Then he took off my trousers and ripped my knickers. As he raped me, his mobile began to ring. I said it was his wife and he got really angry. The phone rang and rang and he finished quickly. He asked me over and over, 'What do you think of me? Do you fancy me?' I wouldn't answer. Eventually I said, 'You're just Rob.' He said, 'I think you're an annoying little bitch. I've had better shags than that.' I'd quickly scrabbled to pull up my knickers and trousers and grabbed my bag and keys, ready to lock him in and go. But as I got to the stairs he pinned me against the wall and said I wasn't allowed to tell anyone. Then he grabbed my throat and asked me to repeat it. He said, 'Promise or I'll take your daughters and do something to them.' So I promised. I got into a cab a few moments later and cried all the way home. I realised then that I had been with Rob for almost an hour.

When I arrived home it was just after midnight and my husband was still up because he had friends over. But I just went straight upstairs. I got into bed with all my clothes on, even my boots. I woke in the early hours in a state of panic and rang the Samaritans. But when they answered I put down the phone. Then I just sat there until morning. I put on a brave face because it was my daughter's birthday. But when my brother-in-law took me shopping for the party I broke down and told him I'd been attacked. He insisted I tell my husband but I didn't want to spoil the party. I changed my clothes but didn't wash. I couldn't bear to touch myself or look at my body. Finally, on Sunday, I told my husband. I'd asked a friend to be there when I did it. He was drinking his tea and threw it across the room. Then he went upstairs. My friend left and I found him crying. We held each other for the rest of the night. But on Monday he was very angry – he'd not been there to help me when I needed him. I called the local rape crisis centre, who urged me to see a doctor because I still hadn't washed, but I couldn't face it. My husband called my two sisters and they took me to a sexual-assault referral centre. I left my husband saying he was going to track Rob down, so I was very distressed. I had an examination and, finally, a shower. I was sure I was fine but the doctor told my sisters that I was in shock. The police came round on the Wednesday and then again and again. In the end it took four weeks on and off to do the statement.

The police arrested Rob at home about a week after it happened. When I hadn't turned up at work on the Monday after it happened he'd called me over and over on my mobile, leaving messages, pleading with me to call him back. When I heard his voice I felt petrified. In the end my sisters took my phone away. The police interviewed all the staff about that night in the bar. They confirmed I'd not been drinking. The police also took pictures of the boardroom and found forensic evidence. He couldn't deny it had happened. So he used consent as his defence. I attempted to go into work a couple of times but had panic attacks. I felt suffocated by everyone looking at me. My GP prescribed me sedatives, said I was suffering from post traumatic stress disorder.

Eight weeks after the attack I took an overdose. I would never have contemplated something like that before. Afterwards I felt angry with myself for doing that when I had a husband and daughters. How could I not have thought of them? I spent two weeks on a psychiatric ward. I felt safe there. They seemed to understand what I was going through and I didn't have to face the outside world. I got out of hospital just before Christmas. My company had contacted my sister to say they wanted me to sign a compromise agreement saying they were not liable for anything. They had paid Rob off and given him a reference. They also made it clear that if I didn't get back to work I'd be jeopardising my job.

Finally, in March, they sacked me. Rob got a reference. I got the sack. In the same month the Crown Prosecution Service decided they wouldn't pursue the case. The detective and officer assigned as my chaperone were flabbergasted. The Crown Prosecution Service said that the text message my friend had sent me that night – saying 'be good' – and the comments I'd made about having an affair would make the case difficult to prosecute. There was nothing I could do. Rob was placed on police bail for six months and his records and DNA have gone onto the police database. So at least if he does do it again and gets caught again there's a greater chance the Crown Prosecution Service will pursue it. But meanwhile he's out there in a new job and my life is in pieces. I have five hours of therapy a week and can function. But I only work locally as a part-time temp rather than going into the city pursuing a career, as I had been. My husband has been very supportive but he's been through the immediate aftermath of the attack and the overdose and I feel I just can't keep talking about it to him. And of course I can't let the girls know how I'm feeling. The result is I feel isolated from my family. I feel so angry with myself. Why didn't I fight harder, scream louder? And I feel angry at him. The career I built up, the family life I knew, it's all been destroyed by him. I can't go back. I have to make a new life from scratch. It's going to be a long process.

Adult male rape

The biggest myth around adult male rape is that it's always a gay crime. 'We had research done recently which showed that a lot of people are convinced that men involved in male rape are gay,' says Sergeant Iain Ferguson, who co-ordinates strategies in community relations in Westminster for the Metropolitan Police. He is also chair of a sub-group of the Independent Advisory Group to Project Sapphire, looking specifically at male abuse and male sexual assault.

'The numbers in recorded sexual crime against heterosexual men may be small but research we have done with support agencies shows that they are getting three times as many cases being reported to them as the Met. And that was only the agencies we contacted. The figures might therefore be higher still.'

It wasn't until 1995 that male rape was categorised as a crime. And according to the joint police and CPS inspectorate report in 2002, since the introduction of the statutory offence of male rape in 1996, there has been an increase in reporting of offences year on year.

In 1996, the number of recorded male rapes was 227; by 1999 it had more than doubled to 504. And between April 2001 and March 2002, there were 735 recorded rapes against males – showing figures have more than trebled in six years.

The biggest and most detailed study yet reveals that 72 per cent of victims of male rape knew their assailants and, of those, 72 per cent had believed their assailant was heterosexual.

'I've been involved with this area of crime for over eight years,' says Sergeant Ferguson, 'and you always hear the same comments – he must have been gay, he must have asked for it, he must have done something wrong... The stereotype that a man cannot be a victim of rape is so strong.'

Survivors UK, the only national support organisation for male survivors of sex crime, had 6,000 calls to their helpline in twelve months spanning 2001 and 2002 from men who had survived child and adult sexual abuse. 'And most of those men described themselves, and the perpetrators, as straight,' says Adam Chugg, the organisation's coordinator. 'Perpetrators included friends, strangers, acquaintances, work colleagues, dates, relatives, male nurses and sisters' partners.

'And yet men always seem to ask themselves, If another man had "sex" with me, no matter what consent was involved, how can I call myself straight?' says Chugg. 'Why was I chosen for the attack? Why did he think I was gay? Am I secretly gay?'

Diana Warren-Holland is director of Portsmouth Area Rape Crisis Service and says they were so overwhelmed by the consistent calls for support they were receiving from heterosexual men that they set up helplines and counselling for them. 'We were getting more and more individuals telling us, I keep getting told about gay helplines, but I'm not gay.

'So in 1994 we extended the service for men. Rape is a people issue. Women are raped but so are children and men. The first year we opened our lines and our doors to men, something like 70 per cent of male callers defined themselves as heterosexual and many of them were in relationships.'

Male rape is about bravado, bullying, power – not sexual gratification. 'The rapist needs to feel strong at someone else's expense,' says Warren-Holland.

Rapes on men take many different forms. There are cases where men are jumped in alleyways and parks by strangers but more often than not rape is by an acquaintance and takes place in a domestic setting.

'It happens abroad quite a lot,' says Adam Chugg. 'A businessmen called us who'd been having a drink in a bar, got chatting to two blokes, left the bar and was followed by them before being raped by them on his way back to his hotel. And it happens to all ages and races. Recently we had a call from a grandfather on holiday with his family and grandchildren, who had been attacked and raped. It can happen to any man, anywhere.'

Talking about the rape and reporting the crime

If a man is in a relationship with a woman, it can be hard for him to talk to her about what's happened. But, whether he keeps the rape to himself or tells his partner, it can cause difficulties for him, for her and for their relationship.

'There are many reactions when partners are told,' says Harry Stoyles of West Yorkshire Victim Support, who alone has seen 24 male-rape survivors in two years. 'If it takes a while for a man to feel ready to talk, some partners cannot come to terms with why they were not told before. They think he has not been honest with them. Others think it's down to them that their partner's been unable to tell them. They feel inadequate.

'Some women will know something's wrong and might push their partner to say something. But this could be damaging. It needs to be the right time for the survivor and the right time in the relationship. Some men tell a woman right at the beginning of a new relationship and not all women can handle this.'

'Women have reported having felt disgusted by what their partner told them,' says Willis James of First Step in Leicester, a support group for male survivors of sex abuse and rape. 'The telling stage is so significant that men often just pour everything out with no censorship, no regard for how it sounds to the other person – who is hearing this for the first time.'

The man might also feel that by telling his partner he's got it all out and that somehow that will put a lid on it, says Harry Stoyles. 'But he needs to realise that his partner will have questions. Is he prepared to articulate all the things she may ask? Writing down in advance what he wants her to know, and including what he feels she might want to know, could help.'

There can be problems with intimacy. Men may think their partners won't love them because they've been violated. 'Some men experience flashbacks whilst having sex with their female partners,' says Willis James. 'Or the sexual act might become something to relieve tension or to affirm their heterosexuality, rather than something that's about love or sexual pleasure. They are desperately trying to make sex normal and healthy again.'

For survivors, the crime not only puts a question mark over their sexuality but it also challenges their maleness. 'It's the old macho image – you're not a man if you can't protect yourself,' says Iain Ferguson. 'The overall effect this crime has on male psychology is a very powerful deterrent for men when it comes to reporting the crime.'

Survivors UK statistics show that only 9 per cent of men report to the police. And according to callers on their helpline, the main reasons men give for failing to report a rape to the police include:

* not knowing that it is a crime

* not wanting to tell

* not knowing how to

* fear of not being believed

* fear of disclosure of sexuality

* concern that sexuality may become an issue

* fear of being accused of committing a crime themselves

* myths about the police

If a male does allege rape to the police, the process is the same as if it's a female. 'If it's in London, men can ask for a male or female police chaperone or express a preference for a male or female doctor to examine them and we will attempt to provide what they want,' says Sergeant Ferguson. 'We're also trying to challenge the CPS and court process as well as encouraging training in the legal profession, the healthcare professions, support agencies and the police.'

Adam Chugg says that the majority of support agencies did not exist, or work with male survivors, as recently as 1995.

'Now the National Association of Services for Male Sexual Abuse Survivors has forty members.

'But we believe that male rape and abuse is probably where female rape was a generation ago. Despite all the evidence, many people want to deny either that it happens at all or that it is as common as it is. Some people refuse to believe a man can be at risk in everyday life. So we still have a long way to go – and particularly in dealing with the "gay rape" notion.

'However, on an individual basis I cannot stress enough that we believe that healing and recovery is always possible.'

'Just as we are trying to do with women, we need to create confidence in the support services and the criminal justice system,' says Iain Ferguson. 'And we need to look at public education. People need to recognise this crime does happen – and that it's usually not a gay crime.'

(For advice on supporting a survivor, see pages 140–2.)

Paul

I'd been out with mates for a stag party. By about two in the morning most of them had gone home and I was really drunk. Me and two of them that were left decided to go to a club. It was really crowded and it wasn't long before I headed for the loos because I felt really sick. Things are a bit blurry but I know I couldn't find my mates when I came out so I decided to head for home. On the way out I met a bloke I knew from work – Mark. We chatted for a bit and eventually decided we'd share a taxi. But when we got to my place Mark suggested we go to his place and carry on drinking. My girlfriend had gone to stay with her parents so there was no one to expect me back and I said, 'OK'. We got to his place and drank until about 5 a.m., when I fell asleep on the lounge floor.

The next thing I remember is being pushed against a chair and Mark entering me from behind. I told him to stop and tried to get away but he wouldn't stop. Eventually I managed to struggle free and Mark was laughing his head off. He said he reckoned I'd enjoyed it. Then he said if I told anyone what had happened he'd say I was gay and that I'd come on to him. I felt sick. I just wanted to get out. But he ordered me a cab and offered to make me coffee as if nothing had happened.

Eventually the taxi arrived and soon I was home. I got straight in the shower. I found the number for St Mary's Sexual Assault Referral Centre in the phone book. I didn't know what I wanted. I just needed to know I was all right. I was terrified people would find out what had gone on. I dreaded seeing Mark at work. I was able to refer myself for a forensic medical exam at the centre but decided I'd store the samples. Not all centres can offer self-referral apparently but I was glad they did – it meant I could check I was OK, have the evidence kept safe, but not have to decide immediately about reporting to the police.

The next day I phoned the centre to speak to a counsellor. I told them that I'd told my girlfriend what happened and that she had suggested reporting to the police. I said I wasn't sure I could face reporting to the police. I felt they'd just take the p— I mean, rape only happens to women, doesn't it? Anyway, they made an appointment for me and my girlfriend to attend the centre the next day so we could explore all the available options. The counsellor talked us through what might happen if a report was made to the police and she also discussed anonymised intelligence information – where you can report without giving details of yourself. In the end I decided to report to the police. I was still worried about what would happen at work and what might be said. But the counsellor described the procedure to report to the police and reassured us about the support and counselling the centre could continue to offer. I didn't get back in touch with the centre until a couple of months later. The police were still investigating what happened and I'd been off sick from work.

Me and my girlfriend were finding it difficult to cope, so the centre suggested we come in separately and see different *counsellors there. I think it's helped us to talk about what we're feeling without the other person there – helped us individually and in terms of our relationship. But we've decided we're also going to go somewhere else for some relationship counselling. It's not been easy.*

5

Drug Rape

Imagine being raped and wanting to escape from your attacker but your body is paralysed. Or you wake up in a place with no idea how you got there and only gradually realise, perhaps through physical evidence like bruising or by disturbing flashbacks, that you were raped. You might even be completely unaware you were raped until some time later – maybe even several years later – when the police contact you with photographs and videos taken by the attacker.

If you have taken drugs or have had alcohol, or both, and are then attacked because you were vulnerable, those drugs aided your attack. But drinking or taking drugs does not amount to consent to a sexual act. This inability to consent is currently recognised in law.

Drugs may also be given without women or men knowing, with the intention of interfering with their memory and their ability to resist. Some drugs can also reputedly create desire and involvement when the woman or man previously showed no sign of wanting either drugs or sex.

This is the stuff of nightmares. But it is also actually the experience of countless women and men – 'countless' because, although there are some statistics that indicate the number of drug-assisted assault victims, experts believe these represent only a very small proportion of the numbers actually experiencing this crime.

The Drug Rape Trust says that in 2000, 2,000 women in Britain reported that they had been sexually assaulted after their drinks had been spiked. This was a rise of 60 per cent on the previous year. They also noted that 11 per cent of victims were male.

The Metropolitan Police, on the other hand, saw no significant increase in drug rape between 2000 and 2002. But DCI Richard Walton, head of Project Sapphire, admits that, 'of course, the under-reporting is probably very high.' And the Drug Rape Trust's Peter Sturman, himself a detective chief inspector in the Metropolitan Police, says, 'We're sure the police figures are the tip of the iceberg.'

The Rape Crisis Federation admit they have had a lot of calls about drug rape, and St Mary's Sexual Assault Referral Centre in Manchester has noted a marked increase in reports of drug-assisted rape. 'We are certainly getting far more women saying they think they've been drugged than we ever have before,' says Bernie Ryan, the centre's manager. 'But the nature of being drug-raped means many people are coming to us too late to have tests or they recall virtually nothing. It's very difficult.'

The fight against drug-assisted sexual assault

The Drug Rape Trust was launched on 1 December 1999 and is the only body specialising in the fight against drug-assisted sexual assault. The Trust conducts research as well as providing support for victims and training and advice for police, prosecutors, magistrates and victim-support groups.

Chair Peter Sturman is a leading world expert in this field and produced a review for the Home Office in 2000 that made 71 recommendations to overhaul the system for investigating these crimes. He has also set up an international exchange of information so tips on good practice for enforcers across the world can be shared.

And in its 2002 white paper 'Protecting the Public', the government made it clear that it intends to increase the maximum penalty from two to ten years for administering drugs to a woman in order to have unlawful sexual intercourse.

Where does it happen and who are its victims?

Clubs and pubs are the most common locations – almost half of people are drugged here. This is followed by the home of the victim or the attacker and university campuses. Around a fifth happen in hotels. Drug-assisted rape also appears to be most common in cities.

The crime seems to occur more often among students than in other sections of the population – but 42 per cent of complainants are in their thirties.

In his Home Office review, Peter Sturman points out that drug-assisted sexual assault has been wrongly linked with date rape. 'Most complainants say they were not on a date,' he says. In most cases – almost three-quarters – the offender is known to the victim.

Which drugs are used?

The Drug Rape Trust points out that there are 67 known drugs on the market that have been linked to this crime. But the purpose of this book is not to provide a 'how to' guide for potential drug rapists. For this reason it gives no specific details of drugs used, their individual effects or where they can be obtained.

What Peter Sturman is keen to point out, however, is that although the drug Rohypnol is repeatedly mentioned in connection with drug rape, a study conducted for his review concluded that it is not the most common drug used in either the UK or the USA.

'Rohypnol was a key drug in sexual assault in the US for a long time and when we first started seeing drug rape here in the UK, we jumped on the bandwagon, assuming it must be as significant as in the US,' says Sturman.

'But Rohypnol has never been detected by the forensic-science service in the UK in sexual-assault offences. We are now making the same assumptions with gamma hydroxy-butyrate (GHB). The danger is that if these two drugs are absent in toxicology testing, then it might be assumed the woman can't have been a victim of drug rape.'

However, since 1 May 1998, it has been a criminal offence to be in possession of Rohypnol without a prescription. This is now punishable by up to two years in jail with an unlimited fine. The makers of the drug have also taken some steps to prevent its misuse. It has been coloured blue, will fizz on contact with a liquid and will float at the top of a drink for approximately 20 minutes after being added.

Alcohol

The majority of drugs used appear to have been mixed with alcohol. But it is important to remember that alcohol is itself a drug and that it is, in fact, the most common drug used.

According to figures compiled by the Drug Rape Trust, alcohol shows up in complainants' samples a staggering 29 times more often than all the other drug-rape drugs put together.

Professor Liz Kelly's 2000 review for the CPS looks at research revealing men's perceptions of women's use of alcohol, especially excessive drinking. It shows that men believe that excessive drinking indicates sexual availability, whatever the woman may say.

'Drinking by women is read as a sign of having a reputation... and [is seen as] a justification for the use of coercion.' Indeed, one study showed that some men deliberately targeted women who would 'fit the stereotype of "asking for it"'. And in another study, based in Ireland, young men admitted that if they were interested in having sex, 'they would target young women who were drunk, or who they could get drunk.'

What effect do the drugs have?

Each drug produces its own symptoms. Cocktails of drugs may also be used and the effects can be enhanced when taken with alcohol. But generally effects can include any or all of the following:

*Vagueness, self-contradiction, inability to explain events in fine detail, inability to describe the suspect or the sequence of events consistently over time. The level of confusion will depend on the drug dosage and the time elapsed since it was administered.

*Little or no memory of what happened. (Loss of memory of events prior to taking the drug may indicate that the drug was given earlier than thought and by a different suspect.) Some memories may come back. Some will not. Perhaps the only indication that it happened are physical injuries.

*Awareness of what was happening but being powerless to prevent it. Drugs and/or alcohol may have caused 'consent' to be given to things not normally agreed to. The body might have reacted to sexual stimulation, no matter how much the mind was rejecting it.

*Suffering trauma.

*Fear of the unknown. For example, asking questions like, What happened? How many offenders were there? Did someone take pictures or videos?

It might help you to regain some of the missing time if you can piece together the facts:

*Where were you when you were drugged?

* Where were you when you first regained consciousness?

* What is your last memory?

* If there were different places involved, how long will it have taken to move between them? Did anyone see you during that time?

* Examine your body. You may be unaware of any injuries or pain.

Emma

It started as a usual Saturday night out with the girls. We were going round the pubs for a few drinks and were having a good time. My two sisters headed home but my friend Evelyn and I decided to carry on to the club. The bouncers were being difficult about letting people in and while we waited we got chatting to three guys. They said they were doctors, looked like they were in their late twenties or early thirties, and said they were visiting the coast on a friend's stag weekend. They told us they were staying in a hotel just around the corner and suggested we join them in the hotel bar for a drink. I was angry we couldn't get into the club and my friend was also very persuasive, so we decided to go. We saw it as nothing more than a drink. We both had boyfriends and didn't find these men remotely attractive.

We sat outside to have our drinks because it was a nice night. But after chatting for a while they started asking if we'd like to go skinny dipping in the hotel pool. This made us feel uncomfortable so we went off to the loo and decided we'd finish our drinks and get a cab home. From this point the whole thing is very blurry for me. We ended up going into the hotel bar and drinking some more. I wanted to leave and asked the night porter to call us a cab but it never arrived. Evelyn went to the toilet to be sick but I never went to check if she was OK –

which is not like me. I recall one of the men took my friend to a bedroom to sleep as she'd passed out. The other two persuaded me to go down to the health club. I remember being in the sauna and two of them having sex with me. Then the third arrived and something snapped. Until then it was as if I was having an out-of-body experience. I knew what was happening but was unable to do anything about it.

I ran out of the sauna, grabbed my clothes and left my underwear. I got upstairs and was crying uncontrollably. They followed me up and I begged them to tell me where my friend was but they wouldn't. I was desperate to leave so I got a taxi.

On the journey I called my boyfriend and told him I'd been raped. He called the police and they turned up at my house shortly afterwards. I was still really confused and couldn't answer the policewoman's questions properly. But she suggested she didn't believe me. Then she went and got my friend from the hotel. My friend later told me she'd said to her in the car, 'Does she often do this sort of thing?'

I went to work the following day, I didn't know what else to do. The police called me there and said I'd need to sign a retraction. But when the policeman met me from work, although I was ready to sign anything – I just wanted it all to go away – he said after speaking to me for a while that he thought I'd been drugged. I've never taken drugs and this hadn't crossed my mind until he said it. I decided to go to the police station for some tests. But the doctor there seemed to think I was wasting his time. He didn't even examine me. And the specialist rape officer talked to me for about three minutes before she said she had to go because she was busy. They also tested my friend and advised we go to the genito-urinary medicine clinic for tests for STIs. The following day I was called by another police officer and told I needed to make a full statement. I didn't feel up to it but she put pressure on me and eventually I agreed she could come to my home for an informal chat. At first she was sceptical but then she went away and researched the effects of drugs known to be used in sexual attacks and agreed my experiences matched those of other women who had been given certain drugs exactly.

Finally, I was taken seriously but it was explained to me that I would have to make a detailed statement, taking the police through my experience minute by minute, and that it could mean going to trial. The three men turned out to be Royal Marines and I was told the story would hit the headlines and be very public. The police seemed to be doing all they could to persuade me not to take it any further. The female police officer was saying to me that the process could take eighteen months and that if it was her she wouldn't go ahead with it. I was in such a state I just wanted it all to end anyway. And I knew that there was a lack of evidence – due to the appalling handling of the case by the police at the outset. But maybe if I hadn't had to expend so much energy fighting to be believed at the beginning, when I felt so low anyway after what had happened, I'd have had more energy to pursue charges. As it was, I couldn't go out, didn't want to leave the house or go anywhere with my friends for at least six months. And it's affected my work at university. But I'm determined this won't continue to ruin my life. I will graduate. They won't win. Evelyn and I are still good friends but we very rarely discuss what happened. I wouldn't have been able to get through this without the support of my family, my boyfriend and my friends. I never thought this would happen to me.

Detection

Over two-thirds of drug-rape survivors realise that they have been assaulted within eight hours. Most have some memories of the attack and these sometimes become clearer over time. In one group of victims of drug-assisted assault, 77 per cent had reported to the police within 48 hours of the attack.

But the delay between the crime taking place and its being reported can cause problems in detection. This is because not only may the victim find it hard to recall details but also because potential evidence both in urine and blood may have disappeared by the time samples are taken.

Drugs are detectable in urine for a longer period than in blood but detection in blood allows for the possibility of determining the dose given. The length of time drugs remain detectable in the body varies depending on the drug, the dosage, the victim's body weight and other factors. Some drugs are detectable in urine up to six hours after ingestion, others up to 72 hours.

It is important that, if possible, you keep the clothes you were wearing and any other items that could be useful for testing. If there are traces of your vomit on anything, for example, this will be of interest to those carrying out the forensics on your case.

Breakthroughs in testing

Early-evidence kits

'We've developed early-evidence kits which are suitable for first response officers to take mouth swabs and urine samples from a victim,' says Mary Newton, serious-sexual-offences officer for the forensic-science service. 'We introduced them because victims were having to wait until a chaperone was found or wait for a medical examination and would go to the toilet in the meantime. If we can capture that immediately with an early-evidence kit it provides the best sample for a toxicologist. But some drugs of abuse will show in urine for up to four days afterwards.

'The kits were launched nationally in August 2002 and within days a third of police forces had ordered them and have since placed repeat orders. They can also be used by police at the front desk in stations and police on traffic patrol.

'But at the moment alcohol is the drug we're detecting most often.'

Hair analysis

Dr Hugh Rushton of the School of Pharmacy at Portsmouth University is one of the leaders in the research into hair sampling. 'It is an area of testing which could be fantastic in drug-rape cases,' he says.

'At the moment we have to take quite a large sample of hair to test but we are working towards needing only one millimetre of one hair to detect a substance. And as long as the hair length is there, we have the potential to find a substance in the hair of a drug-rape survivor years after the rape – no problem.'

'We're looking at detecting a number of different drugs,' says John Wicks, managing director of Trichotech, in Cardiff, a laboratory specialising in hair analysis. 'We are moving towards picking up single doses and even timing in hair samples. We just look at the part of the hair that approximates with the time of the rape. It won't be proof, other supportive evidence will be needed, but it will be corroborative.

'All the people working in this field have made significant advances. It will provide persuasive evidence. It is a crucial area of testing and I have every confidence in its possibilities.'

Unreliable tests

In September 2002 tests designed to detect spiked drinks were withdrawn from sale. The tests, contained in dipsticks and beer mats, were found to be capable of giving a drink the all-clear although it contained a drug.

The Drug Rape Trust is not supporting anything that is currently on the market to detect spiked drinks but it is continuing its research with the government into a swizzle stick.

Drug rape in court

'It is crucial we give weight to what a victim of drug-assisted assault is telling us,' says Peter Sturman. 'We must not assume she's an unreliable witness because she was drugged.

'A murder victim cannot be a witness but we can still achieve convictions for murder. I want to see the prosecution of rapists even when there is no toxicological evidence that a drug has been used. This type of evidence is a bonus but not a necessity. You don't need all the pieces in a jigsaw to see a picture.

'Circumstantial evidence must not be disregarded. Dr Harold Shipman went to prison on circumstantial evidence.

'We have allowed the emergence of a culture where people do not report what has happened because they think they are the victims of a crime that will never be solved, a culture where we are sending a message to the offender that says, Carry on, you'll never be caught, you've got the perfect crime in a pill.

'But we are not allowing this situation to prevail any longer. We are now getting convictions. This is not the perfect crime.'

Graham Laskey, 49, and his brother Simon, 38, were given sixteen life sentences between them at Swansea Crown Court in October 1999 for drugging and raping women over a 20-year period. They crushed drugs into the women's tea before attacking them.

Dennis Fenton was jailed for twelve years at Antrim Crown Court in Belfast in 2000. The cocktail of chemicals Fenton slipped into his seventeen-year-old victim's drink was so powerful that she was unconscious for 24 hours. During that time 42-year-old Fenton attacked her and took photos of her semi-naked. Tests later showed she had been given a huge dose of drugs. An RUC spokesman said the case proved that drug rapists could be caught, with the co-operation of victims – even if they couldn't remember anything.

Nurse Kevin Cobb raped women after drugging them with a powerful sedative used in minor surgery and was given seven life sentences in July 2000; and DJ Richard Baker, who was jailed for life in June 1999 for a string of sex attacks, had his pockets stuffed with pictures of unconscious naked women and packets of drugs.

In September 2002, a family doctor was jailed for twelve years after pleading guilty to sex attacks on child and adult patients. Timothy Healy, 57, from north London, drugged some before videoing himself abusing their unconscious bodies at his surgery or his home. The victims, two aged eleven at the time, others in their teens and twenties and all male, were unaware they had been assaulted until police traced them in 2001. The court was told his victims were mentally scarred by what had happened, speaking of their 'anger', 'disgust' and 'degradation'. One attempted suicide. Eleven attended court.

Millie

I was visiting my friend Vikki in the city where she lived and we decided to go out at about 5.30 p.m. to a bar in a very nice area. Vikki had just bought a flat, so I got a bottle of wine for us to celebrate. The next thing I knew was I was waking on the sofa in Vikki's flat at 3 a.m. I found Vikki in her bed and woke her. Both of us knew something wasn't right.

I was having flashes of memory but they seemed like daydreams – of walking down the bar's stairs, of the bouncers making chauvinistic comments as we left. Vikki remembered us being in an area we shouldn't have been. I could recall grass, linking arms with Vikki and her pulling me to the ground as she passed out. Then my legs went from under me.

At some point we must have been separated. I remember an overwhelming feeling of fear. Then there were three guys, I think, and with that memory comes this sense of sheer panic. I know that on some level I knew something very dangerous was happening. I can remember breathing slower and slower. I thought I'd been brought home in a white van and had been asked questions like, What's your name and where do you live?

The next morning we called the police to ask if they'd brought us home the night before and we called the bar. They said we'd been asked to leave for being drunk and disorderly. But CCTV cameras later showed Vikki and I walking off down the street and we were certainly not 'disorderly'. The timing on it also showed that it was before 7.30 p.m. We knew one bottle of wine would not have had the effect they claimed.

We went to the police station later that day to make a report. We took in the clothes we'd been wearing. Both of us had heavy bruising on our inner thighs, Vikki on her arms, too, and I had terrible aching between my legs. And although she was living with her boyfriend, I wasn't in a relationship and hadn't had sex in a while. The police decided from the evidence we gave that there was a strong likelihood that drugs were involved but they concluded that no rape had occurred. So they sent us home.

At first we were relieved. Perhaps nothing had happened. But after a while we knew we were deluding ourselves. I tried to go to sleep that night but every time I lay down I had this overwhelming sense of fear. I drove home the next day and reported what had happened to my own police. By then the bruising and aching were worse. Within ten minutes they had a specialist officer with me asking me far more specific questions than the other police had. She said it was my choice but she would suggest I have a medical examination. I agreed and went to a nearby sexual-assault referral centre. The doctor there concluded that I had been raped. She said there was fluid inside me and the bruises were pressure bruises. The trouble was I'd had several showers by the time I had that exam – no one had felt we'd been raped and we couldn't remember – so a lot of evidence had probably been lost.

My police force called Vikki's and they took her in for a medical exam, plus they fingerprinted her flat and took away some items for forensic testing. But her exam didn't include an anal exam, checking under her nails, measuring bruising, or taking any hair – all of which they'd done with me – and they said it was inconclusive. Four days after the rape photos were taken of my bruising – which included definite fingerprint bruising.

I live alone but my assigned specialist officer took me to see my family and explained to them what had happened. It was awful to see all these people close to me getting so upset. I myself just felt numb. For four weeks I couldn't sleep properly. I kept getting the feelings of panic. Vikki and I were interviewed again at my parents' home a few days later by officers from her area. It was horrible to have to go through all the questioning again. Plus there was a lot of sexual innuendo from the police questioning us. It was also confirmed that a police van had picked me up but despite my initially seeming dead, my breathing being so shallow and me subsequently experiencing breathing difficulties – obviously a side effect of the drugs we'd been given – I was not taken to hospital. Instead I was dumped in a wheelie-bin shed outside Vikki's flat until I could gain access. The police in Vikki's area told me two versions of events, the second one not mentioning my physical condition at all. I've since made an official complaint.

I had tests for STIs and for HIV and all were clear. I no longer have contact with Vikki. She didn't have counselling, her relationship ended and she had a series of destructive ones after that – and began to drink heavily. Our friendship broke down because we took very different routes after the rape and she didn't want to do what I had. I had fifteen sessions of counselling, beginning two weeks after the attack, at the sexual-assault referral centre where I had my medical examination. The benefits were huge for me. It helped me deal with my feelings, to accept that I won't remember what happened and I started to be able to sleep again.

The investigation has not reached a conclusion yet. There have been problems with the forensic evidence and it's having to be retested. The police later said they thought the bar and the bouncers were in collusion, spiking drinks and tipping off attackers. What happened to us when we left happened two days later to two girls in the same bar. They were taken to hospital with exactly the same physical symptoms – the paralysis and the breathing difficulties . . . But the police talked to the bar about their suspicions and it didn't happen again.

Making a complaint against the police where my friend lives has not been easy. I have only been able to to do it because I've had the support of my own police and the centre where I had counselling. It's hard because the process means I'm constantly having to talk about what happened, to relive it. But it's been my choice to make the complaint and that makes me feel very strong.

I've had a relationship since the attack and it was fine. It's now ended but that was a natural end – not because the rape was an issue.

Everyone handles things differently but to me there was never a choice about reporting. And despite my treatment I haven't a single regret about that.

I still get flashbacks. They're not visual, I just feel unbelievably frightened – it suffocates me. But they're happening less and less. I don't even think about the rape every day any more. I no longer feel I'm a rape victim, I'm me but just to have this thing that happened in my life. It's no longer everything.

6

Rape in Relationships and After They Break Up

When someone you love, whom you trust, whom you have chosen to be a large part of your life, rapes you, it is a betrayal that destablilises your whole life.

The shock of it may lead you to attempt to make sense of it quickly. This can't have been rape – you've been together so long, he told you he cared about you, this is the father of your children, maybe you're making too big a thing of it.

If it keeps happening you might begin to feel, often with encouragement from your partner, that it's your fault, that you deserve it. You might also feel there's nothing you can do about it. Perhaps your partner has threatened you or those you care about. Or you, and others, may rely on him for your financial security.

But rape is never any woman's fault. And coping with rape in a relationship is particularly complex. No one should ever think it is as easy as just walking out of the door.

Being made to have sex without consent is defined in law as 'rape' but it is often only when physical forms of coercion are involved that we and the criminal justice system seem to accept that a rape has taken place. Indeed, American research has shown that using the word 'rape' greatly decreases the reporting of forced sex. The redesign of questions in the US National Crime Victimization Study in 1992 to refer to forced sex rather than rape resulted in findings four times higher than previous versions. Even now it does not use the word 'rape'.

'Women see rape when they are in a relationship with someone as sex gone wrong rather than as an act of violence,' says Jackie Clark, Manager of the REACH (rape, examination, advice, counselling, help) centres in Newcastle and Sunderland. 'If their partner used a knife or a fist there would be no confusion – the only difference here is that the penis is the weapon. But being with someone does not mean you sign over the right to your body.'

How many of us are relationship-rape survivors?

Whether it's mental cruelty, threats, actual violence with injury or rape, it has been shown that at least one-quarter to one-third of all women will experience violence from a partner in their lifetime.

The most recent British Crime Survey to look closely at rape appeared in 2000 and found that a staggering 45 per cent of reported rapes were by a partner. While the Rape Crisis Federation has found that 55 per cent of women contacting them were repeatedly sexually assaulted by the same man. 'This highlights that rape and sexual assault are not necessarily isolated incidents in women's lives,' says Lynne Harne from the Federation. Indeed, in one survey of victims of domestic violence, almost three-quarters of women said they had been raped up to five times in the previous year.

Your life may be at risk

These attacks are highly likely to result in physical injury, are second only to stranger rapes in terms of the presence of a weapon and they are more likely to be repeated than attacks by any other perpetrator.

The lives of women who are raped by their partners, particularly after separation, can be in severe danger. The violence is often life-threatening and can include murder. Home Office figures show that up to a third of murders of women are committed by present or ex-partners. Yet despite such alarming findings, marital rape is still not taken as seriously as stranger rape by the police and courts.

In fact, until as recently as 1991, rape in marriage was not against the law. 'The marital-rape exclusion' protected it from criminal prosecution. This dated from 1736 when Lord Chief Justice Matthew Hale stated that 'the husband cannot be guilty of rape committed by himself upon his lawful wife, for by their mutual matrimonial consent and contract, the wife hath given up herself in this kind unto her husband which she cannot retract'. In other words, it was not possible for a man to rape his wife because she belonged to him.

It took over 250 years for this to change. It was not until July 1990 that a husband was accused of raping his wife. And the House of Lords precipitated a change in the law in October 1991 by refusing to apply the marital-rape exemption. They stressed that the time had now arrived, 'when the law should declare that a rapist remains a rapist and is subject to the criminal law, irrespective of his relationship with his victim'. It was not until even more recently, in 2000, that Northern Ireland saw the first conviction for marital rape when Lord Justice Campbell sentenced a man to seven years at Downpatrick Crown Court.

Who rapes his partner?

According to 'Young People's Attitudes Towards Violence, Sex and Relationships', a study of young men between the ages of 14 and 21, one in seven thought it could be OK for a man to force a woman to have sex if they had been going out for a long time. One in five considered it acceptable to force a woman to have sex if she were his wife.

It is a myth that different types of men rape their wives or partners than those who rape strangers. Homicidal rapists sometimes kill their wives as well as women they know less intimately. Frederick West was charged in 1994 with killing thirteen women. He tortured and raped many of them, including his wife and daughter. John Duffy, a homicidal rapist, charged with raping and killing three women in 1990, also raped his wife before they separated. Richard Baker, a serial rapist who worked as a nightclub DJ, raped women he dated as well as those who were strangers to him.

Jenny

We had only been with each other for ten weeks when he first hit me. Paul was convinced I was seeing someone else, smashed a partition wall, kicked in a door and then slapped me. I screamed at him to get out, that we were finished. He pleaded with me to let him stay until he found another flat. Days passed and he insisted it wouldn't happen again. I convinced myself it was a one-off, stupidly believed a slap wasn't as bad as a punch. So he stayed. I was infatuated with him. I felt it was love at first sight and after a week I didn't want to spend a minute away from him. But within a month he had raped me. At the time, because I wasn't physically hurt, because it hadn't been brutal like it can be for some women, because it was him simply forcing me to do something I didn't want, I didn't see it as rape. He didn't need to use violence to rape me. I was terrified of him. But he'd made me equally terrified of him going. Even that early on he'd got a real hold on me. He'd chipped away at my self-esteem. He'd convinced me that everything I had, everything I was, was down to him.

Then we moved to Ireland. My family said it was too much too soon. I was only eighteen. But I just rowed with them until we weren't speaking at all. My partner was from Ireland so while he was returning to friends and family, I was leaving mine behind and on bad terms. I would be completely isolated. But

I was sure the man I'd fallen in love with would reappear once he was 'home'. Then on our first night there, staying at his parents' house, he raped me again. After a month we got our own flat. At least once a week he'd punch me in the back of the head, kick me or strangle me. He often packed my bags and threw me on to the street. But I couldn't bear to contact anyone in England. I didn't want them to know, to say, Told you so. I thought about approaching the police but even if they arrested Paul they might not be able to detain him – then he'd come looking for me and I'd end up six feet under. This would all go through my head as I stood outside. Then he'd bring me back in, saying, I told you you couldn't survive without me.

I got pregnant in December 1998 and he hit me a lot for the next nine months. I was so relieved to finally give birth to a healthy boy. I called him Conor. But Paul wasn't at the birth. It's often recommended that couples wait six weeks before having sex following a baby. And six weeks later to the day he raped me. I had post-natal depression but Paul wouldn't let me take the drugs. He told me constantly that Conor had ruined his life, that it wasn't too late to give him up. When Conor cried at night I'd bring him into bed with us and Paul would elbow him in the stomach. I begged Paul to hurt me instead but I think he knew it hurt me more to see him rough our son up.

For a year I tried desperately to make things work. I wanted Conor to have a dad and mum together. I asked Paul, Where's the person I fell in love with? And he told me, It was all an act. Finally I realised, this man was not going to change. It was January 2000 when I first told anyone what had been going on. It was Paul's sister. We'd become very close. But all she said was that I was a fool for staying. I was devastated. Each day I believed this might be the one Paul would kill me and part of me wished he would. But my son deserved a better life than to be brought up by that monster. I had to leave. I started to pack away our belongings, telling Paul I was just sorting out old clothes or needed to put things out of reach of our inquisitive toddler. I also tried to keep back tiny amounts of money.

Then in May I finally told my mum. I walked the streets with Conor for ages before I finally managed to dial her number on my mobile. I just cried and cried. At last I managed to get my words out and I could hear my mum was fighting back tears. But she stayed strong and told me, *If you want to leave him, we're here for you.* Then she told me to get straight to Citizens' Advice. When I explained the situation to them I was shaking like I've never shaken before. They said they could get me into a refuge in a few days' time and that, using a special fund, might eventually be able to get me home to England.

But the next day I went back and asked to go to the refuge immediately. Now I'd decided to leave I couldn't stand the pretence, smiling at Paul when all I wanted to do was to put my hands on him and really hurt him. And that's when they told me they might be able to get me and Conor on a plane to England that day. I was told I had half an hour to pack everything I needed to take, then I'd get a police escort with a taxi to the station. I was terrified Paul would come home early and see me but I managed to do it. But Paul had seen me in the taxi on his way home from work and must have told his family because before I'd even reached the station they were texting me that they'd protect me, asking me not to take Conor. I just switched off my mobile. At the airport check in I was told my son was not on my plane ticket. I only had fifteen minutes before we needed to board and went mad. They tried to calm me and pointed to another desk where I could get help quickly. But when I turned to find the desk, Paul's mum, dad and sister were walking towards me. They told me Paul was sorry, that he wouldn't do it again. I yelled that he was an abuser and that I was not going to be a punchbag any more. I wanted to cause a fuss so lots of people noticed us, so Conor and I would be protected by being conspicuous. They were trying to take the pushchair but I gripped it tightly in one hand and dragged the trolley with our cases with the other. Finally I had Conor's ticket in my hand. As I checked in my bags, I asked Paul's dad, 'Why didn't anyone ever stand up for me?' He started crying but couldn't answer.

As I headed for the departure lounge I knew they couldn't touch me any more. At last I was going home. I was ecstatic. But I was also crying so hard I could barely breathe. When I got to Gatwick and through customs, the sliding doors parted and there were my mum and dad. I hugged them for ages. For the next week Paul called my mum and dad's house at all hours of the day and night. Finally I saw a solicitor who gave me a number for a domestic-violence helpline and another for a refuge. My mum and dad really didn't want me to go but I couldn't allow them to be subjected to that harassment.

I rang the refuge and was told they could get me in the next day, which was great. But I was also really scared. I'd heard they were horrible places with damp rising up the walls and broken furniture, full of drunk women with screaming kids on their hips. So when one of the refuge staff came to collect me in the evening I expected the worst. But when I arrived the first thing I noticed was how quiet it was. Then I was shown to my room and I was overcome with relief. It was a newly furnished bedsit with a proper little kitchen. I had even been left some food to tide me over. Conor was asleep so I settled him with all his familiar teddies round him and then I just cried.

The staff at the refuge were so supportive. There was a meeting every week to discuss how you were feeling physically and emotionally and to talk about your goals. And that could be something as simple as a short walk to the shops alone. Conor had friends for the first time in his life and while he played in the garden at the back with the other children I was being helped with my income-support and housing-benefit forms. Everyone was so friendly, it really was like being part of a large family. I had constant waves of fear that kept sweeping over me that Paul was going to find me and kill me but I was constantly reassured by the fact that no men were allowed to *call and there were no male visitors. He wouldn't find me there. At least I was safe. I've got a prohibitive-steps order to stop Paul or anyone taking Conor out of my care and also a residency order. Paul still calls my parents occasionally but he can't touch us now.*

After six months at the refuge I'm about to move into a maisonette that's only a short bus ride away from my parents. Being at the refuge reminds you contantly that you're not the only person to have gone through this and that really helps. After three years of isolation I no longer feel alone. I will really miss the refuge and all the friends I've made but we'll keep in touch. They're setting up a group for current and ex-residents. I feel ten times stronger than I did when I arrived six months ago. Good things are really starting to happen for me. The staff have encouraged me to do so much I feel really empowered. I would not be this strong if it hadn't been for them. I'm so lucky I've been helped to get a second chance. I can do whatever I want with my life now. No one can hurt me now.

Reporting to the police

Of women raped by their husbands, 91 per cent of those surveyed in the 1991 study 'Wife Rape, Marriage and Law' had never reported or discussed the matter with any official agency.

And the 2002 joint report from the police and CPS showed that in cases where victims withdrew their complaints, more than a third featured rape by a partner or former partner. This reflects the difficulties faced by rape victims when they're making a complaint against an offender on whom they may depend both economically and emotionally. There is, of course, also the potential for victims to be intimidated, either directly or indirectly, by their current or ex-partner, into withdrawing the allegation.

How can the law protect you?

Civil action

A restraining order

You could consider making an application for a restraining order. Under the Protection of Harassment Act, harassment is a criminal offence and the restraining order carries with it a power of arrest.

A power of arrest means the police officer attending an incident should immediately arrest the perpetrator and take him into custody to be brought before the court as soon as possible. A restraining order can be applied for by anyone, regardless of whether there is a family-type relationship.

The most effective remedies an individual can take, if she is in a family situation, and a power of arrest is desired, are under the Family Law Act 1996. These are as follows:

A non-molestation order

Anyone who has been abused, threatened or assaulted by someone with whom they are living or have had a family-type relationship is able to apply, as an 'associated person', for an order prohibiting further molestation. This protects you from violence, threats of violence and harassment and can also protect your children. If you have been the victim of physical violence and the court is concerned it will happen again, the judge should attach a power of arrest to the order. The non-molestation and non-occupation provisions not only apply to spouses, ex-spouses and (heterosexual) cohabitants, but also between siblings, parents and their adult children, or homosexual partners (where there is or has been cohabitation) and some other blood relatives.

A non-occupation order

It is also possible to apply for an order regulating the occupation of the home, which includes the exclusion of the offender.

The legislation does not extend to those who have never lived with their abusers, except where there has been a formal promise of future marriage, or there is a child for whom both are parents or have parental responsibility. A homosexual partner can apply for an occupation order only if she or he has existing rights to occupy the home (for example she or he is a tenant or owner).

While other injunctive remedies are available for women who are in this situation, they are not as effective because a power of arrest cannot be attached.

Recently there has been increasing concern among solicitors about the difficulties of obtaining Legal Aid to pursue applications for injunctions. This follows the introduction of revised criteria for the granting of funding for applications for injunctive protection. There appears to be variance in the way these principles are applied, with some Legal Services Commission (formerly Legal Aid) offices requiring a warning letter to have been sent to the other party – a measure that women might feel reluctant to take for safety reasons, or a report to the police to have been made, which again women may feel reluctant to do.

Karen Dovaston, chair of the Domestic Violence Sub-Committee for the Solicitors' Family Law Association and a solicitor specialising in these cases for Martin Nossel in Essex, says that if women have concerns that their partners will find out they've made an application for a non-molestation order and will attack them physically before it is served, then it is possible to make an emergency application.

'In this case you can get a "without-notice order" that can be served before the other party is informed,' says Dovaston. 'I had a client who was in an emergency situation with her husband, who came to see me at 5 p.m. I worked on the case overnight, I was in court first thing the next morning and had the order in my hand before 11 a.m.

'There are also measures which can be taken to keep a woman's address confidential if she is fleeing a partner who is a threat to her, although at the moment these rely on your solicitor's creativity.'

Women need to be aware that there may be limits in terms of funding but should talk to a family-law solicitor for guidance on this and on which remedy best suits their particular circumstances. 'Help is there and it can be turned around very quickly,' says Dovaston.

For details of accredited specialists in family law, contact the Solicitors' Family Law Association (see page 212). Its members do emergency work as well as providing information and guidance on a less urgent basis.

Criminal law

If your case goes to court

The closer the relationship between the defendant and the complainant, the more difficult it is to gain a conviction. In one case of marital rape the defendant had admitted the assault to the police, but the CPS decided not to bring a prosecution. They argued that there was 'very little likelihood' of the man reoffending and that charges would not be in the public interest.

Cases involving marital rape receive significantly lower sentences than those involving rape by strangers. A comparison of sentences for different types of rape in 1999 showed that in cases of stranger rape the average sentence is 10.7 years, whereas in cases involving wives the sentence falls to 6.7 years. And in cases of relationship rape, the average is only 4.1 years. For couples who still live together, shorter sentences seem to be the rule – and there's a good chance of that sentence being reduced on appeal. In 1986, Lord Chief Justice Lane introduced new recommendations for sentencing in rape cases, called the Billam guidelines. Billam suggests that when rape has taken place in the victim's home, sentencing should start at eight years. Yet in 1999, relationship rape was receiving sentences of only half this length.

In June 2002 a package of proposed measures was announced by the government to improve the situation for victims of domestic violence. It was suggested that restraining orders be introduced which courts could impose during sentencing to ensure violent men stay away from their partners, either in addition to, or in place of, a custodial sentence. A new criminal offence of breaching a non-molestation order – the orders granted by civil courts to stop an abusive ex-partner harassing a woman – should also be introduced. Such an offence already exists in Northern Ireland.

Caron

I was sixteen when I started going out with him and he was nearly twenty years older. He never gave me a choice about what we did in bed and I never wanted any of it. Sometimes I'd protest. I'd be crying my eyes out. But he'd just say, Take the pain. Those words echo around my head even now, eight years later. I ended up on anti-depressants, which made me really drowsy. I'd wake in the night in this drugged state and he'd be having sex with me. I was with him for two years before I finally told him I wanted to end the relationship. Then he stalked me for seven months. I was terrified. I knew what he was capable of. I was so relieved when I moved away to go to university. Although he stalked me whenever I was home on vacation or to visit my parents. When he could no longer exert his power over me in bed he did it like this.

It took about four years before the enormity of it all hit me. Then I just went down and down until I ended up in hospital. I was suicidal. I was on medication and needed therapy until fairly recently. I still have a problem with sex. I haven't had many partners at all but those I have been intimate with I've had to explain why I'm in such a state, why I'm so scared. And in my current, long-term relationship it has certainly been an issue.

Recently I decided to report to the police. It was so difficult. It brought it all to the surface. I felt he'd find out and come and get me. I had an examination and the police took a statement. I wasn't expecting anything to come of it in terms of a case for me. So much time has elapsed. I did it for my self-worth and for other women. My complaint is on file now so if other women report him to the police . . . and I strongly believe it will happen to someone else. I've now completed my master's degree and I have a job. It's a long process but I feel I'm finally becoming part of the world again.

Supporting a victim of any form of domestic violence, including rape

As friends, relatives, neighbours or colleagues, we have a crucial role to play in supporting someone we suspect is, or know is, in a domestic-violence situation. 'So often we believe it is a private matter, that what goes on behind closed doors is none of our concern,' says Sandra Horley, chief executive of Refuge, which offers national support for victims of domestic violence.

'We might also be frightened. Abusers very often threaten or even attack anyone who attempts to intervene.' Or we might find it hard to believe abuse is even going on. 'The men who abuse can be intensely charming and charismatic and present a likeable face to the rest of the world.'

At the beginning of the relationship the man praises his partner but once she makes a commitment his behaviour changes, alternating between abuse and begging forgiveness, smothering her in affection and promising her he will never behave badly again. But a woman in this situation is not causing this abuse. Contrary to what he may be telling her, it is not her fault. Changing her behaviour will therefore make no difference.

If we respond inappropriately then we could do considerable damage and leave the woman at greater risk. It's important to realise our limitations. But there is a lot we can do that may ultimately provide the spur a woman needs to seek help.

It can be very difficult when, if you try to talk to a woman about her situation, she appears ambivalent about leaving. But this is such a complex and sometimes long-standing situation that even realising that leaving might be better than staying, let alone deciding to actually leave, might be a very gradual process. 'We should never judge a woman for staying or for going back when she's left,' says Sandra Horley.

'To present an instant solution, saying, "You should leave" is wrong,' says Horley. 'What you can do is help the woman find options and help her consider them in turn. A woman can't be expected to recreate her life overnight. She has to make her decision in her own time. Reassure her that finding a solution takes time and effort but it is possible.

'Acknowledge the negative and the positive in her abuser. Don't run him down. It will only have the effect of making a woman feel worse. She will think, I chose this bad person. And she may well shut down. Talk about the good in her partner but also stress that he is not entitled to be violent. It is against the law.'

Ask the woman what he has said will happen to her if she leaves and take what he has said seriously. There is a strong chance her abuser will carry out those threats.

'You can and should offer consistent emotional support,' says Horley. 'Encourage a woman not to blame herself. Help her see that changing her behaviour will not stop this man being abusive. Tell her that reaching out for help, revealing what is happening, is nothing to be ashamed of. It is a brave and positive step. Congratulate her on her strength and courage in surviving this abuse. And act as her advocate, pass on information, tell her about agencies who can offer her support.'

The time may come when the woman can no longer tolerate the situation and has to leave immediately. You should make it clear that you can be there for her in whichever way works for her and keeps her safe.

Have numbers ready for support agencies, her family doctor and the police. Tell her in advance she can use your phone and help her be aware of the nearest call boxes. Let her know she can stay with you if she needs to escape in a hurry. Ask if she'd like you to telephone the police if an emergency occurs. Suggest to her that she have a spare set of house keys cut and leave them with you. And offer to keep important papers for her – passports, birth and marriage certificates, child-benefit books, cheque or building society books. Have everything in one place so that she can reach documents quickly.

And Sandra Horley stresses that we should never under-estimate the role the police can play. 'Arresting and charging an abuser is one of the most effective deterrents to domestic violence. It shows him the consequences of his behaviour, shows him that what he's doing is against the law. And it shows the victim that she does not have to put up with it.'

DCI Sue Williams specialises in domestic-violence issues for the Metroplitan Police. 'If we respond to a call and there are no apparent offences we will still record it as a non-crime incident. And even if the victim later withdraws her allegations it will still be on record. This means we are building up valuable intelligence. This might not only help a victim in any criminal proceedings but can also help if she is, for example, making an application to be re-housed.

'Even if there is not an incident in progress then you can still call and a specialist police officer from the local community-safety unit will make contact with the alleged victim to offer support, provide referrals and give advice. The officer will conduct a risk assessment and if they identify the victim is at risk from further harm, they will take appropriate action for early intervention and provide a safety plan.

'The officer will investigate any allegation or incident to obtain the best evidence. And if the victim is reluctant to press charges then the officer can refer them to a support agency or offer advice on how to take civil action and apply for a court order or injunction to protect themselves or their children from the abuser. Some support agencies will also assist the victim with this.'

Signs to look for

*There is no typical victim, any woman can be at risk.

*Have you noticed that the woman's partner is jealous and possessive? Does he accuse her unjustly of having affairs and try to prevent her from having contacts outside the home?

*Does the man lose his temper over trivial matters?

*Does his behaviour alternate from charming and loving one minute to angry and abusive the next?

*Does the man blame her for all the problems in the relationship?

*Does she become over-anxious if she is not home to receive his telephone calls or greet him from work?

*Is she isolated and dependent on him – has she stopped socialising?

*Does she behave differently when her partner is present – from being friendly and sociable to becoming withdrawn and inhibited?

*Most importantly, does she say she is afraid of her partner?

Do and don't

*Never try to patch up the relationship. Violence is not the result of poor communication between the man and woman.

*Be patient and listen. An abused woman is often unable to walk away from her abuser without conquering fears and feelings of guilt that at times seem insurmountable. So it doesn't help her to have someone constantly telling her that she should leave without a second thought.

*You may mean well in wanting to tell the woman that she is crazy for staying but this will only intensify her confusion and lack of self-esteem.

*Criticising her partner also does not help. The woman may leap to his defence or feel that there's something wrong with her for choosing the wrong man.

*Never ask what she did to provoke him. Assure the woman that she is not to blame. She is not responsible for her abuser's behaviour.

*Do all you can to boost her self-confidence and courage. Tell her how well she's coped, emphasise her strength, show her that she will be able to survive without her partner.

*Make her aware of agencies she can turn to for help if and when she leaves.

Alisha

We met in May last year and for three months had a great time going out clubbing and just chilling. Then, just after I graduated from university I discovered I was pregnant.

By then Karim and I were living together in Leeds and we had a massive argument. He wanted me to have a termination and when I refused he slapped me across the face so hard it knocked me over. I wanted to leave him but then I thought, I'm going to have a baby, my family are strict Muslims and I knew they wouldn't approve. But I felt I needed support. He'd stolen my mobile so I couldn't get in touch with friends, with anyone. Where else could I go? So I stayed. Karim physically abused me every day. He took my keys and wouldn't let me go anywhere without him. He slapped and punched me – once so hard it knocked teeth out. He spat and urinated on me, kicked my pregnant stomach and, on New Year's Eve last year, he put a knife to my throat and burnt me with his cigarette.

A couple of weeks later, when Karim asked me to borrow some money from my sister, I finally saw a chance to escape. I went to my sister's house. They hadn't seen me for months and suddenly I arrived bruised and burnt. When I told them what had been going on they were in tears. I was shaking with fear because I knew Karim was expecting me back but also so relieved to have got away, to know I had support. He turned up at the house after four days of voice mails threatening to injure my family, burn down their houses and kill me. I called 999 and when the police arrived and arrested Karim they discovered he was concealing a ten-inch kitchen knife. My sisters persuaded me to go with them to the police and tell them the full story.

He was put in prison but when our son Jonathan was born, soon after Karim came out on bail in March, I was back with him. I hoped the baby being there would make a difference but he beat me with his weights and made me cut myself to prove I loved him – threatening me that he'd stab the baby if I didn't. I escaped to my sister's but went back again. I wanted to believe he loved me and Jonathan and would stop. My sisters were desperate to do something. They visited me at our new flat to try to show Karim I had support, hoping it might discourage his abuse. And when I said we were looking for a lodger to help with rent one of them immediately offered to move in. But he wasn't having that.

Karim asked his friend Sean to move in instead – but he was as keen to help as my sisters. Sean stepped in to protect me many times, even though Karim threatened him. And when Karim raped me and then went out overnight, which he did on several occasions, I'd be crying and Sean would comfort me. He kept telling me I should get out and that he'd help however he could. Another friend of Karim's, Neil, moved in nearby and had a clear view into our living room. He saw Karim beating me up and said I could use his mobile any time I needed it. Neil was taking a big chance getting involved. He knew what Karim was capable of but he was prepared to do it. By then Karim was hitting and abusing me five or six times a day. And he'd started to hit Jonathan. When Karim said he wanted me to borrow more money from my sister I saw another chance to escape. And this time I knew I wouldn't be going back. Karim sent Sean with me but we'd discussed my plans and he took me straight to the police station.

The police went to collect the baby and later arrested Karim. Jonathan is now five months old and I'm in a refuge. Karim is in prison, awaiting trial. He has twelve charges against him and could get up to eight years. Sean and Neil took big risks to help me and my sisters never gave up – by taking me to the police, by visiting me and even offering to move in when Karim could have turned on them. And although I know they got frustrated that I kept going back to him, they made it clear I would always have a sanctuary at their house – despite Karim's intimidation. I am now in a refuge, and without my sisters, Sean and Neil I would not be there. Knowing I had people there in the background helped build my confidence. I had to reach the decision to leave for good myself but without those people I don't know how long it would have taken me. I wonder if I'd have ended up dead before I felt strong enough to do it. It's so important to have people there for you, reassuring you, supporting you. It reminds you that you are worth better than this abuse. It helped give me the strength to get out – and to stay out.

Sexual abuse in lesbian relationships

'It's only in recent years that this has been talked about, even in the gay community,' says Petra Mohr of Survivors of Lesbian Abuse. 'Often women call us and they're not even sure they're calling the right line. So I ask them to describe the behaviours they're experiencing. Are they being coerced into something they don't want to do in a sexual context? If they say they are then I can put a name to it, I say, You are being sexually violated. This can be the first step in dealing with the situation.'

Society knows about men raping women, says Mohr. 'Even if they are not fully aware of the extent to which it's happening. But if you're experiencing something no one talks about at all, that people don't even realise goes on ... Women tell me, I haven't heard about it happening to anyone else. It must be my fault.'

'Even if people do take the time to acknowledge it, they think it's weird,' says Mohr. 'They ask, How can a woman do so much damage? Why couldn't you defend yourself? But as is so often the case in male rape or even in heterosexual rape, it's about the power dynamic, not physical strength.'

Talking to someone is a step in the right direction. 'But as with any domestic violence situation, if you've been manipulated over time you lose yourself. You need support in getting that self back, in shifting your focus from trying to please your partner. But, again as with all domestic violence situations, you have to make any changes while at the same time being mindful of threats your partner has made. They could be empty but it's not worth taking the risk. It's just unfortunate that many women are in the worst place before they start to think of doing something.'

When your relationship ends

Both marital rape and marital murder tend to occur when a relationship is breaking up or shortly after the couple have separated. Being raped by a partner can be the thing that convinces a woman she has to leave the relationship or rape can be revenge on her for going. Ending a relationship with a violent man places a woman at particular risk for her life.

'Break-up rape happens in a significant number of relation-ships,' says chartered counselling psychologist Susan Van Scoyoc, clinical director of The Women's Practice. However, as with rape within a relationship, because women find it so hard to acknowledge that this is rape, it is chronically under-reported. 'But awareness is improving. So although rape in relationships is by no means a new thing, I am now seeing increasing numbers of women who actually describe themselves as the survivor of break-up rape – up to one in five of my clients.'

In 'Wife Rape, Marriage and Law', a study of women in eleven different cities in the UK, divorced or separated women were the most likely to be coerced into sex by their ex-husbands. One in three divorced women, compared with one in seven women living with their partners, said they had been coerced. Divorced or separated women were also seven times more likely than married women to have had violence threatened. Of those who said they had been hit and raped, 51 per cent were divorced or separated.

'When women leave men it is', says Sandra Horley,' the ultimate challenge to their authority and they'll do whatever they can to claw back the power they feel they've lost.' The man will often try to be remorseful, to persuade his partner to return. If this does not work he might stalk her, use extreme violence or rape her. 'They do not like the transfer of power – she is taking control of her life and they lash out.'

'I think that women look at this particular form of rape and think it will never happen to them. But they shouldn't,' says Susan Van Scoyoc. 'Statistics have shown repeatedly just how common it is. But because women don't want to talk about it, let alone report it, other women don't realise how much it is going on.'

'Many women who have been sexually abused by their partner feel defiled and humiliated and it is often hard for them to talk about their experiences,' says Sandra Horley. 'He has violated their sense of closeness and trust.'

Amy

I met Paul at university. We were the same age and moved in together in the city when we graduated. We had a great relationship and a great time. But after six years together I felt the spark had gone. One evening in our flat I explained to Paul why I felt things weren't working between us. He was really upset. He kept saying, 'Why are you doing this to me? We're fine.' I hated to see him like that but I'd been feeling this way for six months. He just wouldn't listen so I left to stay with a friend. He called me constantly at home and at work. He kept telling me how bad he felt, asking what he could do to make everything OK again.

Eventually Paul seemed to accept what I was saying and agreed the relationship had come to an end. And two months after I walked out, we arranged for me to pick up the rest of my stuff from the flat. We had a drink first and got on really well. Then we went back to the flat and he helped me get everything together. But as I went to leave he got upset, said I didn't realise what it had been like for him since we'd split, that he'd been suicidal. I told him I hadn't wanted to hurt him and tried to calm him down. But as I went to open the front door he flung me across the room on to the sofa. Then he shouted, 'I'm going to make you feel as bad as you've made me feel.' I was terrified. I thought he was going to beat me up. But then he got on top of me. I struggled, trying to resist, telling him to get off me, but he just held me down. Then he raped me. As he did it, I kept asking myself, How can he do this to me after all that time together and in the flat we shared? Afterwards he got up and said, 'Right, that's it. You can go now.' For a minute I lay there. I couldn't speak. It seemed worse than if a stranger had raped me in the street. I thought I'd known him. I trusted him. My stuff was still by the door and I just picked it up and left.

My friend suggested I go to the police but I couldn't face it. I knew Paul had a temper, he'd argue with me and get worked up but he never threatened me, he was never violent. I thought, I told him I didn't want to be with him any more and he changed into that. It's my fault. I didn't go to work for two weeks. I told my boss I had flu. I thought about contacting Paul. I wanted to ask him, Why did you do it? But I couldn't. And he's not got in touch with me. Paul deserves something after what he did. But how seriously would the police take it? He'd been my boyfriend for six years. I've started counselling. But it's only three weeks since the attack. It still hurts so much. Paul has ruined all the time we spent together. If I'd been in a violent relationship, although it would still have been horrific, perhaps part of me would have known I might be raped. I genuinely didn't ever think it would happen to me.

Breaking up

'It's important to stress that although there may have been no physical or sexual abuse in a relationship, it's likely there'll have been control emotionally or verbally preceding a rape,' says Sandra Woodward, who manages Juniper Lodge, a rape referral and counselling centre in Leicester. 'But at this point of crisis – and that may be when the woman tells him she wants to leave him or later when his anger has festered – the man will need something new to reassert his ability to intimidate. And rape is a very powerful tool.'

*It's unlikely that break-up rape comes from nowhere.

*Your partner may not be hitting you but might be controlling you, by restricting your social life, putting you down in front of people, by his mood swings or by getting angry/withdrawing affection or attention when you don't do what he wants.

*There will be a pattern to this behaviour. But even if you're not consistently feeling wounded, humiliated or frightened and plan to break up with your partner, be cautious.

*Break up at a time and in a place where you can easily get help if necessary.

*Don't return alone to collect belongings. Take a man who won't be aggressive – it changes the balance of power.

*If your ex turns up on your doorstep day or night don't open the door. He may start crying and telling you how much he loves you but he can change quickly, especially if he's been drinking.

*If your ex is persistently harassing you, speak to the police. Tell them you are fearful for your safety. They should visit your ex to warn him off. In most cases this should help.

And, if you have survived break-up rape, Sandra Horley cautions against attempting to make sense of it. 'You may never understand why your ex raped you. What's important is that you put all your energies into your own needs.'

Susan Van Scoyoc says that it is easy to say what needs to be done to reduce the incidence of break-up rape. But in a country where rape in marriage only became illegal in 1991, achieving it is a monumental task. 'Women are becoming increasingly aware that this type of attack is rape and is a crime. But men need to realise it too.'

Sally

I met Mark at the financial consultancy where we both worked. He was ten years older than me and it was my first serious relationship. He was very protective of me, possessive I suppose, but I found that flattering. He hit me a couple of times soon after our first anniversary. But I waved it away. I was barely bruised. But then he started putting increasing pressure on me to do certain things in bed that I really wasn't interested in. It ended up dominating our time together until finally, after two years together, I arrived at his flat from work one day and told him I was leaving.

Mark instantly became violent. He smashed my head against the wall and repeatedly punched me in the stomach and breasts. I was terrified. This wasn't like the odd slap he'd given me before. He seemed to have totally lost control. Then he pushed me to the floor and raped me. He screamed at me and he whispered, and it was the whispering that frightened me the most. He told me, 'I'll make sure you never leave.' I could see in his eyes that he wanted to kill me. He continued to whack me around the head, to pummel my stomach and threw me down the stairs. Then he came down and raped me again. After that I lost consciousness. When I came round I was alone. I have no doubt that Mark had run away, thinking he'd killed me. But somehow I managed to drive back to my flat.

I was treated for concussion, broken ribs and internal injuries. When I returned to work after two weeks I told my boss I'd fallen down the stairs. I was seeing Mark all the time at work but the only way I could cope with that was to completely shut down. I developed depression and had crippling flashbacks several times a day and at night. I couldn't accept that the man I'd shared two years of my life with, who I'd loved and trusted, could have been capable of doing this to me. After a year of this I saw my GP and was diagnosed with post-traumatic stress disorder. Then I began a course of medication and counselling.

It was over three years after the attack that I finally managed to tell my parents and my current partner, whom I've been with for nine months. They've all been very supportive. My flashbacks are less frequent and I no longer need medication. But what happened makes trusting anyone difficult. I always think that I'm going to be 'hurt' if I upset someone. Sex is a real problem for me but I'm hoping that will change in time. I've moved hundreds of miles away from my ex because I'm still so frightened of him. I still have this sense of utter disbelief that this happened to me. I never dreamt he would react like that. He could have killed me. I have some days where I don't think about what happened at all and I realise, My whole life could be like this. I know I've still got a long way to go but I'm determined I'm going to get there. He won't ruin my life any more.

7

Holiday Rape

Whether we go away on business, for pleasure or both, large numbers of us are now travelling overseas. But for most of us, making a trip abroad means only one thing – a holiday. It's the chance to get away from it all and have a great time.

Yet recent reports suggest that for increasing numbers of British women, fun in the sun is the last thing they experience when they become the victims of rape.

Figures compiled exclusively for *Cosmopolitan* by the Foreign Office revealed an alarming number of sex attacks on female holidaymakers abroad. In 2000 and 2001 in Spain, Greece, Turkey and Cyprus, a staggering 94 British women were raped. And the situation seems to be getting worse.

In Greece, incredibly, there were six times as many rapes in 2001 than in the year before. In Cyprus, the figures more than doubled in a year and they also increased in Turkey. And while the number of rapes in Spain decreased in the same period it still topped the league table of the number of rapes of female British holidaymakers.

But these figures are only the tip of the iceberg. 'We cannot stress enough that these are only the rapes which we hear about,' says Sarah Dring, head of Consular Policy at the Foreign Office.

It is shocking enough that only an estimated 10 per cent of UK rapes are reported, but the numbers of unreported sex attacks overseas are believed to be far worse. 'The trauma of rape for women on holiday is obviously magnified,' adds Sarah Dring. 'With the language and cultural barriers and women who are raped perhaps not getting treated as well as they might have done in the UK, many women decide to put it behind them and get the hell out.'

In September 2002 a Greek Cypriot diver, who confessed to beating and raping a 22-year-old Lancashire woman near Ayia Napa, appeared in court under tight security. Zenon Mastrou, 26, was expected to be remanded in custody until an inquiry was completed. He admitted attacking the British tourist before discarding her in a desolate field where she nearly succumbed to her wounds. 'Only wild beasts could have done what happened to this girl and there are people who now want to lynch this man. The authorities will demand that he remains detained until the investigation is over and he is formally charged,' said police spokesman Stelios Neophytou. 'We are still looking for two other suspects connected with the assault.' The woman, from Blackburn, was believed to have been bundled into a car outside a disco in the resort before being driven to the remote spot. In testimony to police, the arrested diver said he had used a wooden implement to beat her. The woman underwent extensive surgery but doctors said her injuries were such that it was possible she would never fully recover.

In June 2002, in Faliraki, Rhodes, Greece, a twenty-year-old woman from Scotland said she was initially seduced but then raped by a middle-aged Greek taxi driver who suggested she give him sex in return for a taxi ride. And a nineteen-year-old woman from the Home Counties claimed she was raped by a 26-year old from Epsom, Surrey, in his Faliraki apartment in the early hours. The man is alleged to have confessed to the police and apologised to the girl, who went on to drop all charges when she learned that she would have to remain in Rhodes until the court case was heard.

There had already been seven reported attacks on women in Faliraki that year. The month before, one holiday rep was raped and two were assaulted at knifepoint. In 2001 there were ten reported rapes, of which six involved British girls.

Police and the British consul in Athens met in 2002 to discuss ways of tackling the problem. And the Foreign Office reviewed its travel advice for Greece saying, 'Personal attacks, including sexual assault and rape, are infrequent. However, there have recently been a number of widely reported incidents of sexual assault and rape on some Greek islands. Visitors are advised to maintain at least the same level of personal security awareness as in the UK. We strongly advise lone visitors, especially females, never to accept lifts from strangers or acquaintances at any time.'

What do I do if I am a victim of sex crime abroad?

*If you've been attacked and you don't know where the police station is, head for an upmarket hotel. They should have English-speaking staff and know of a female doctor.

*Contact/go to the British consulate or embassy. A member of staff will accompany you to the police station and arrange for an interpreter, they can arrange for you to see a doctor and can tell you what to expect from the local police and judiciary. The consulate will help you contact family and friends and assist with your return. And before you return to the UK, the consul will also put you in touch with counsellors experienced in dealing with rape victims. Your travel company will have details of the location of the consulate or embassy. Or you can get the details before you even leave home by going on to the Foreign Office website (see page 214).

*Speak to your holiday rep and/or contact the Association of British Travel Agents (ABTA) (see page 214).

Can I wait until I get home to report?

DCI Richard Walton, head of the Metropolitan Police's Project Sapphire, says that women must report a sexual assault in the country where it has taken place. 'We cannot lead a rape investigation when it's taken place overseas, only assist with it.'

What can I expect when I report a rape overseas?

Many police forces abroad have an attitude to rape that is very different from the one women can expect in the UK. 'Unfortunately, many countries do not see rape as a crime,' says Richard Walton. 'Consequently, they handle things in a totally different way – which might not always be regarded as desirable.'

It therefore does not surprise him that, while the numbers of women becoming the victims of sexual assault overseas appear to be increasing, crime in this area is hugely under-reported. 'Police stations in holiday destinations can be desperate places,' he comments.

The Association of British Travel Agents agrees that many countries do not take sexual assault as seriously as the UK. 'But holiday reps are trained to be sympathetic and to liaise with the police – in fact, to put pressure on them if they are not doing all they should,' says Sean Tipton of the Association of British Travel Agents.

'If there is not a British consulate where you are, call the British embassy,' says Sarah Dring. 'They have a network of honorary consuls who will be just as helpful when it comes to reporting to the police.' And she points out that the Foreign Office regularly runs targeted campaigns to increase awareness for particular groups. Spring 2003 will see us advising 18–30 clubbers. 'We're always concerned when a case is highlighted and we're constantly looking to see if there's more we can be doing to alert people to the dangers. Directly we're aware of crime, we put it in our travel advice on the website.'

The Foreign Office website offers travel advice for every country in the world. It is regularly updated and includes specific guidelines for female travellers. 'For instance, it helps to be aware that drug-assisted rape is a growing risk in some countries. In certain destinations date-rape pills are becoming more and more common,' says Dring.

Anna

When I ordered two cocktails at a local bar for me and my friend Sarah on our first evening in Faliraki, Rhodes, last year I had no idea the drinks had been spiked.

Sarah went home at midnight after drinking half her cocktail but I had the lot. I was dancing so I told her I'd follow her in a few minutes. And that's the last thing I remember – before I came to on the beach lying on a sunbed with someone having sex with me, watched by another man, at about 4 a.m. I pushed him off me and ran down the beach. I became quite hysterical when I realised I had no memory of how I'd got there. But some people found me, calmed me down and took me back to Sarah, who was asleep on her bed. It took us ten minutes to wake her.

We told the holiday reps. We also reported it to the police but they had no interest, let alone sympathy. Sarah tried to get someone at the hospital to examine me but they refused. The hotel owners told us that a girl staying there a few weeks earlier had also been raped on the beach and another had been raped in one of the clubs. And a local who worked in the hotel told us that he'd heard of a barman who was offering holidaymakers the girls they wanted for money. We booked the first flight home we could. I've travelled all over the world and this was the last thing I expected in a European resort. Women need to know that rape on holiday is a real threat.

What can I do when I get back?

Talk to the police
You need to have reported the crime in the country where it took place but the police in England and Wales can assist you and police overseas.

Contact Victim Support
Do this via your local police or by checking in your local phone directory. You can also contact the Victim Supportline (see page 203). 'The effects of rape can be compounded when it happens abroad,' says Tamara Wilder of Victim Support. 'We urge victims to contact us when they return to the UK but they very often don't get easy access to victim support in other countries. We are aware of this and are certainly looking into changing this situation.'

Get in touch with the Association of British Travel Agents
Francis Duke, of the Association, insists that all holiday reps have a duty of care. 'They should respond in a professional but also sensitive way. Certainly they are trained to do so. But if they don't, you should complain to the tour company afterwards. And if you're not satisfied with their response then the Association offers a low-cost arbitration service.'

Ring the Rape Crisis Federation
It will put you in touch with a rape crisis group in your area and can provide support to any woman raped here or abroad. 'It's important to remember that rape is experienced by female tourists in Britain as well as by British women overseas,' says Irene Murray of the Federation. 'If you've been raped abroad we can provide help with technical details of reporting rape that has happened in a foreign country, including getting in touch with the Foreign Office.'

Bea

I was attacked in Tenerife and left for dead on the roadside. I did report the incident to the police, but they didn't manage to catch my rapist while I was out there. When I got back home, my family and friends were anxious that I saw a rape counsellor. I know this is an important part of recovery, but as I fortunately can't remember much about the actual attack, I didn't feel the need to talk to anyone. What I find really hard to deal with is the fact the police seem to have done nothing to catch the man who raped me. I am liaising with the police in Tenerife but my attacker still hasn't been caught and he may well have attacked again. When I went on holiday I had the same attitude as most girls – that an attack would never happen to me. Now I know how vital it is not to put yourself at risk.

Ceri

When me and my friend Emma arrived in Cavos, Corfu, we found the lock on our hotel room door was faulty. But the rep said he'd sort it out later in the day. After a day by the pool me and Emma went back to our room to get ready to go out. But I was so tired I fell asleep in my bikini on the bed. Then Emma left the room. I woke in confusion when I realised someone was lying on top of me. It was a bloke and he was trying to pull off my bikini bottoms. I kept shouting, 'Who are you?' But he just kept snatching at my bikini, pulling and pulling with one hand while he tried to hold me down with the other. Finally, he lost his temper and yelled, 'I met you in the airport. I was talking to you.' In one rush it came to me that this was a bloke who I'd noticed in the departure lounge, in reception when we were telling the rep about our door lock and by the pool that day. He was just staring at me. He'd really given me the creeps.

I wrenched my knees up to my chest and shoved him off me and off the bed. I ran to the door and struggled to get it open but it wouldn't budge. I told him he better not try anything else, my friends would be back any minute. I was throwing things at him but he just walked slowly towards me, laughing. Then he grabbed my two wrists, trying to hold them tight in one hand while he put the other over my mouth and shoved me against the wall. I struggled and fought but he threw me on the floor. Then I heard Emma outside with one of the lads from earlier and I yelled out. My attacker jumped off the balcony on to an adjacent roof and ran off.

The holiday rep took a statement but said there was nothing they could do until I found the man who attacked me. Five days later, I hadn't left our room. The lock remained broken and all my appeals to fly home or at least be moved had been refused. I was finally persuaded to go out and saw my attacker but the rep I called said he could do nothing that night.

The next day they turned up at my room and told me that if I went to the police the bloke would be thrown in a Greek jail and that I wouldn't be allowed to leave the country. And they added that if it went to trial and he got away with it, I'd go to jail. I called my mum and she immediately spoke to the tour company but they just fobbed her off. So she contacted the British consulate and they told the tour company they would be liable if they didn't get a translator and take me to the police to report the crime – and that both me and my attacker needed to make statements. The hotel manager had overheard me on the phone and personally walked me down to another hotel and found me a room there.

Finally, the reps found my attacker in a room on another floor of my original hotel. But when we got to the police station it was a waste of time. My translator was a taxi-driver friend of one of the reps. I was eventually put on a flight home but, apart from the local police taking a statement from me and Emma, I've heard nothing since. I had no idea of the law or my rights. Everything the reps told me was wrong. There was no one I could turn to for advice whom I could trust. I had to give up my job in a bank when I got back. I just couldn't cope. I had just wanted to lie on a sun lounger with my eyes closed and not worry about anything for a week. Instead somebody tried to rape me and nobody cared.

Things to think about before and during your holiday

'Women need to take the same level of care overseas as they would at home,' says Sarah Dring. And Melanie Capper of *Lonely Planet* agrees. 'Have more fun than you would here but don't act in a way that you wouldn't here. Don't think, It's just a one-week package holiday to chill, I'll be fine.'

Before you go

*Visit the Foreign and Commonwealth Office website or telephone the travel advice unit (see page 214) for the latest details of the country you are visiting and for the contact details of the local British embassy, high commission or consulate.

*Check the Thorn Tree section of the Lonely Planet website (see page 214). It is a travellers' forum, where people can report personal experiences or things they've heard have happened in a particular area.

*Look at guidebooks. All books in the Lonely Planet series have, for instance, a specific section on women's safety.

*Avoid booking a flight that arrives late at night, especially if you are a first-time visitor to that country. These are often cheaper but safety is not worth saving money on.

*Spend a bit extra on a hotel in a decent area: the streets will be safer at night; there'll be more security in the hotel; and single women will get less hassle. Or at least try to book your first night's accommodation beforehand, so you don't find yourself stranded.

*Find out, and check, important numbers before you go (many guidebooks will include them) and if you forget, when you get to your destination, make sure you find out the number for directory enquiries. But this should be a last resort – language could be a problem.

When you're there

*Ask your rep if there have been any attacks locally or if there are areas you should avoid. But don't rely on reps to tell you everything. Explore the area where you are staying thoroughly by daylight. It's important to get your bearings and know the dodgy parts to avoid.

*Find out how you can get hold of your travel company in an emergency.

*If you're taking a taxi, use only registered or government-run ones. If you don't know which they are, go to one of the upmarket hotel chains and get the staff to call one. Check the driver when the taxi arrives and trust your instincts as to whether you take the taxi or not. If the driver is OK, take his number and use him again.

*Ask staff the best place at your destination to be picked up from for the return journey. And make sure you know how to pronounce the name of your hotel, and its exact location, so you're sure you'll be taken straight back.

*Don't ever assume the only threat is from the locals. Don't be lulled into a false sense of security because you're with a group of British tourists.

*Even if there are a lot of other tourists around, wearing skimpy clothes or sunbathing nude will draw unwelcome attention to you in most cultures. And if you're on your own, you'll be vulnerable.

*If you want a big drink, stick to the hotel bar. You won't have to negotiate unfamiliar streets while drunk.

*If you're in a café or bar, read. Sitting 'people watching' shouldn't put out 'on the pull' signals, but it can.

*If you're constantly approached don't freak out and scream at people. It could make things worse.

*Wear sunglasses. The less eye contact you make, the fewer approaches you'll get.

*Stick together. Look out for your friends, try not to split up and watch each other's drinks.

Irene Murray of the Rape Crisis Federation says that the Federation is keen to develop links with travel agents in order to inform them of how they can support women who experience rape abroad – this includes the British Tourist Board.

'The Federation is also currently working with nineteen other European Rape Crisis groups to develop a European website for information on rape-crisis services.' This is being carried out by the newly developed European Network of Rape Crisis.

'We are endeavouring to link to its website as many international rape-crisis websites as is possible in order to offer women the opportunity to have access to rape-crisis services globally.'

She believes that more needs to be done for women experiencing rape while on holiday or on business abroad. 'We would like to see improved practice in this area. There needs to be some standardisation in practice in these circumstances, particularly in gaining access to justice. Women need this information.'

8

The Aftermath

How a woman reacts when she is raped depends on many things. She will have had her own preconceptions about rape and, if she tells the people close to her, their attitude to rape will affect her too. The amount of positive support available to her can be vital. And the circumstances of her rape, her character and her emotional health prior to the rape are also crucial.

If she reports the crime, the treatment she receives here will also be important. Reactions may not always be positive. Again, judgements may be made – because it is rare for there not to be some sort of blame attached to the woman who has been raped and for the woman herself not to feel guilt.

Susan Van Scoyoc, clinical director of The Women's Practice, says she is constantly seeing fear, doubt and guilt. 'Women wonder, Did I give out the wrong message by what I said, what I did, what I wore? Again and again I hear, I must have done something wrong.

'It's this guilt which enables a lot of sex crime to continue because it makes women keep it a secret. But women should not wake up the next day and feel guilty about something someone else has done against their will.'

However you react to being raped, your response is never wrong. However you cope is right for you. 'Rape has a huge impact on your life,' says Anita Hobbs, counselling supervisor at the Women's Counselling Service in London. 'Its effects can be catastrophic emotionally, economically and physically. And a woman needs to make her own choices about what's best for her in dealing with that.'

'You were a victim, there's no doubt about that. There was a loss of control. But you can choose no longer to be a victim,' says Lucia Hall, a therapist specialising in trauma and abuse. 'How long are you going to let that person be in control? You had no choice then but you do now.'

The psychological effects of rape and/or sexual abuse

According to a report on rape by the Royal College of Psychiatrists in 1996, victims of rape describe feeling 'contaminated, unclean, almost untouchable afterwards'. It points out that the experience may also destroy everything the victim previously relied on with regard to 'safety, trust, sexuality, intimacy and the predictability of the future', leaving them with 'a sense of being fundamentally changed . . . of loss, as if a part of oneself . . . has been destroyed.'

Clinical psychologist Linda Blair stresses that women often take a long time simply to get through the numbness following rape. 'They might not even begin the process of reacting to what's happened for several months. And if they don't fully grieve for that self they have lost then, even years later, exposure to a situation that reminds them of what happened before can knock down the protective wall they've constructed. For that to happen after so long with no apparent reaction to the rape can be quite scary.'

Rape-trauma syndrome

This was first described in the 1970s and is now regarded as a variant of post-traumatic stress disorder (PTSD). Studies have shown that the symptoms of a post-traumatic stress reaction are present in the majority of rape victims for several weeks after the assault. However, these and other forms of distress resolve themselves quickly so that three months after the assault, even without any form of support, most victims no longer meet the criteria for PTSD. But the Royal College of Psychiatrists caution in their 1996 report that 'even for rape victims who appear to have recovered, future exposure to stresses (such as the trial) may cause an exacerbation of symptoms or a relapse.'

The rape-trauma syndrome is composed of three stages: the acute stage, the outer adjustment stage and the re-normalisation stage.

The acute stage

The immediate symptoms may last a few days to a few weeks and may overlap with the outward adjustment stage. Behaviours that may be present in the acute stage are:

Diminished alertness, numbness, dulled sensory, affective and memory functions, disorganised thought content, paralysing anxiety, pronounced internal tremor, obsession to wash, hysteria and confusion, bewilderment, acute sensitivity to the reaction of other people. Not all survivors show their emotions outwardly. Some may appear calm and unaffected by the assault.

The outward adjustment stage

Survivors in this stage seem to have resumed their normal lifestyle but there is internal turmoil which may manifest itself in any of the following behaviours:

Continuing anxiety, sense of helplessness, persistent fear and/or depression, mood swings from relatively happy to depression or anger, vivid dreams, recurrent nightmares, insomnia and wakefulness, loss of concentration, physiological reactions such as tension, headaches, fatigue, general feelings of soreness or localised pain in the chest, throat, arm or leg. Specific symptoms may occur that relate to the area of the body that has been assaulted. Survivors of oral rape may have a variety of mouth and throat complaints, while survivors of vaginal or anal rape have different physical reactions.

Words, smells, sounds or phrases may act as a trigger for flashbacks – a memory that can feel as real, and can be as frightening, as the original experience. Flashbacks can occur at any time and anywhere. Some rape survivors self-harm during or after a flashback.

Survivors may experience appetite disturbances, such as nausea and vomiting, or an increase in appetite as a result of 'comfort eating'. They are also prone to developing anorexia and/or bulimia.

A survivor might minimise her experience or block out thoughts of the assault from her mind or consciousness. She tries to block it out completely, to push it out of her mind, but the assault continues to haunt her.

The rape often upsets the woman's normal routine of living. Some are able to resume only a minimal level of functioning. They might withdraw from contact with friends or relatives or with the abuser – or may confront him. They might stay at home and venture out only if accompanied by a friend, be absent from work or drop out of school or college. Others go to work, school or college but are unable to be fully involved. Or they may overcompensate and become very involved in work in order to complete the blocking process.

Guilt is one of the major feelings in rape survivors. It may lead the woman into self-destructive and/or self-abusive behaviour, including self-mutilation – scratching or burning herself, for example – and suicide attempts.

Some survivors develop very suspicious, paranoid feelings about strangers. Some feel fear of everyone. They may feel hesitant to enter new relationships, especially with men, and may become distrustful of existing relationships with men.

Sexual relationships become disturbed. Many women have reported that they were unable to re-establish normal sexual relations and have often shied away from sexual contact for some time after the rape. Some report inhibited sexual response and flashbacks to the rape during intercourse.

The woman may develop dependency on alcohol, cigarettes or drugs, both prescribed and illegal. Phobias are also a common psychological defence – a fear of being in crowds, of being left alone anywhere, of going out at all (agoraphobia), and/or specific fears related to the characteristics of the assailant, such as a moustache, curly hair, the smell of alcohol or cigarettes, type of clothing or car.

The woman may feel rage about the rape, often without feeling there is any way of channelling this rage positively. This may be exacerbated if she has, for example, reported the rape and the assailant has not been caught, or is not prosecuted or is given a very light sentence.

The renormalisation stage
In this stage the rape is no longer the central focus of a woman's life. Guilt and shame become resolved and she no longer blames herself for the attack. For a time pain is evoked if the memory of the attack is revived. After more time passes, the pain loses its intensity. Memories of the attack are no longer constant. It is unlikely that this stage will be reached without effective professional counselling.

The effects of rape can last many years, yet there are often expectations from those close to a survivor that she should recover within a set time. But recovery times vary significantly from one survivor to another, and, in the process of healing, there may be times when a woman is overwhelmed by the pressure of memories and painful emotions. The support a survivor receives can be crucial to her recovery.

How can you support a survivor?

*Help her to deal with the practical consequences, for example, if she is injured take her to the nearest accident and emergency department. She may want you to go with her to a clinic so she can be tested for STIs or for you to buy her a pregnancy test.

*Believe what she says.

*Do not be judgemental, for example, by saying she was drinking too much, wearing certain clothes, behaving in a certain way that provoked this or made her vulnerable.

*Also, do not be judgemental if she didn't fight back or scream or try to escape. She is probably asking herself why she did not do these things and is perhaps feeling bad about it. Don't make things worse.

*Reassure her this is not her fault. The blame is all with her attacker.

*Do not expect her to react in a certain way – the way you feel she should react.

*Try to control your anger or violence at, or your sadness about, what has happened. Expressing your feelings will only add to the trauma. It's understandable for you to feel this way but don't become the one who needs support or comfort. This puts pressure on the victim. If she sees how this has affected you, it may add to the guilt she is perhaps already feeling. She'll feel she has caused this. Try to seek support for yourself elsewhere.

*Allow her to talk or to stay silent. She may feel embarrassed recounting the details or not wish to upset or hurt you. Suggest she speak to a support group. It's often easier talk to strangers. Do not take this personally. And if she does talk to you, be prepared to hear distressing details.

*If she wants to cry, let her. It may be upsetting for you but can be important in the healing process.

*Be available to listen whenever she wants to talk. She might feel she's going on, she's wasting your time. Reassure her this is not the case.

*Do not encourage, or discourage, her to go to the police. This must be her decision.

*Don't tell her to forget it or, some time later, say she shouldn't be crying. The effects of rape can be long-lasting.

Your partner has been raped

*Try not to feel rejected if she does not want intimate contact with you.

*Be patient and offer non-sexual comfort and support. It may be temporary or last for a long period.

*Never put pressure on her. Let her be in control when it comes to intimate and sexual contact.

*It may be difficult to accept your partner has been raped. She will not have wanted to be raped or enjoyed it. Do not suggest by what you say or do that she did. Tell her you do not believe she was to blame and help her to blame the rapist.

*Don't tell her to forget it or put it behind her, to move on. Say you'll be there for her, if you can be sure you will.

(For information for male survivors of child sexual abuse, see pages 28–9; and for male survivors of adult sex crime, see pages 77–83.)

Getting support

A woman who has been raped needs reassurance that her feelings about it are normal and that it is possible to recover. Counselling allows her to explore difficult and complex reactions she may be experiencing, it can help her to restore self-worth and offers her the support she needs to move on. Support services can also present your options, provide information and help in the areas of medical care, housing, education and employment, as well as reporting to the police and proceeding with a case.

Here is a selection of services and support agencies you may wish to use. Contact details of these, and other services and agencies can be found in the Help section at the end of this book.

Counselling and therapy

Some rape-crisis centres, most sexual-assault referral centres, Victim Support and individual counsellors, therapists and psychologists will be able to provide psychological and emotional support for rape survivors. The British Psychological Society website has a 'find a psychologist' section with a register and directory of chartered psychologists. The police and GPs can also put survivors in touch with appropriate counsellors.

'It can be hard to cope with emotional problems alone and it's often difficult to share your feelings easily with someone close to you,' says Linda Blair. 'So it can be beneficial to talk to someone who's "safe", who's not part of your everyday life.'

Blair suggests that if you feel simply that you need someone to listen to you then counselling could be a good idea. 'But if you're also suffering from depression, or have any other psychological problems – for example, agoraphobia, an eating disorder or compulsive behaviours – then it might be wiser to opt for therapy, which can offer guidance in addition to careful listening and reflection. Counsellors and therapists should both offer empathic listening – that is not sympathetic, "I'm superior to you" but equal listening,' Blair explains. 'The Counsellors and therapists should also both offer an accurate reflection of rape survivor's problems. A therapist goes on from there to offer "recipes" for going about solving problems.'

'Our society is still strongly influenced by the idea that people who have suffered ought to develop a stiff upper lip and get on with life,' says Lucia Hall. 'But you are not a failure because you seek help, you're not weak. A lot of people feel like you do. We need to get rid of the stiff upper lip. It minimises people's pain.'

'Survivors working in isolation can get back part of their lives but they need someone else to really make a leap on the path to recovery. Seeing a specialised counsellor is the best way forward,' says Anita Hobbs. 'You only know your own experience but a counsellor or therapist can help you look at your situation in a different way, to step outside your experience.

'But you should not go for counselling because people say it will be good for you. You have to want to do it. Many women who have been raped come to us in a defensive mood but that is not because they don't want to be helped. It's because they have been very hurt. And they may feel nothing can change. You may have become very depressed and it takes a lot of courage to change.'

Bernie Ryan agrees. 'Reactions to rape vary and may include feelings of self-doubt and self-blame. Counselling should aim to allow clients to air their feelings about the events and to explore issues sensitively in order that they can dispel their own myths and stereotypes – which could be adding to their feelings of self-blame and guilt – and promote change.

'This can be frightening. However, clients often have a capacity to change how they live and to survive a crime of this nature.'

'The rape will never not have happened but the way you see it can alter,' says Anita Hobbs. 'It's never too late to get help. I see women making great changes.'

The Rape Crisis Federation
There are 45 rape-crisis groups across England and Wales. You can call the Rape Crisis Federation head office to find your nearest rape-crisis group, look in your local phone directory or contact your local police for their number. 'At a minimum we offer a confidential telephone helpline service for women who have survived anything from sexual harassment to sexual abuse to rape,' says Lynne Harne of the Federation. 'Women

who call can expect to be believed, to receive non-judgemental support and to be given further information. The focus is on the choices and empowerment of the individual woman, rather than telling her what she should do.' You might just want to ring once to ask a question or you may wish to call on a regular basis. Groups can give information on reporting to the police, court procedures and criminal-injuries compensation claims as well as about medical issues, such as pregnancy testing, abortion or sexually transmitted diseases. Some will be able to accompany women to a police station, court, hospital or special clinic. Depending on resources, some groups also offer survivor groups, face-to-face counselling and support for the parents, friends and relatives of survivors.

The Rape and Sexual Abuse Support Centre (RASASC)

This all-woman organisation offers a free helpline service, which is the only one in the country open 365 days a year. It gives support to women and girls over thirteen who have been raped or sexually abused. On the helpline they give the names of other organisations for face-to-face counselling in your area, if that is what you want, or they provide telephone numbers of other agencies, from lawyers and housing to women's organisations.

'Usually, one of the first steps towards recovery is being able to talk and talking anonymously to someone at the end of a phone seems to help, especially those who have been raped or sexually abused some time ago,' says Yvonne Traynor the centre's service director. RASASC offers help to family and friends of survivors and sends lists of reading material as well information to survivors to help them understand that anything they are feeling is normal. From July 2003 they will be offering face-to-face counselling and from November 2003 an advocacy service for women wanting to report the crime and go through the criminal justice system.

'We will also accompany women to hospital, ensuring that they receive the best possible treatment and understanding,' says Traynor. 'If a male survivor calls we will support him on the phone, because we understand how difficult it must have been for him to make the call, and then give him telephone numbers of male organisations for him to contact.'

Sexual-Assault Referral Centres (SARCs)

Women can refer themselves, or be referred by their GP or the police, to these centres, which offer specialised facilities for sexual-offences examination and for counselling.

St Mary's Sexual Assault Referral Centre in Manchester

St Mary's was established in 1986 and provides a comprehensive service to female and male adults in Greater Manchester who have experienced rape or sexual assault at any time in their lives. The centre was the first of its kind in the UK and is nationally and internationally acclaimed as a model of good practice. Services are offered on a 24-hour basis, regardless of whether a report has been made to the police, including 24-hour telephone support, staffed by fully trained crisis workers; forensic medical examination; emotional and practical support; one-to-one counselling for clients and their supporters; screeening for HIV and STIs; and support through criminal proceedings and compensation claims.

The Haven in south London

The Haven is a dedicated sexual-assault referral centre based in the Department of Sexual Health in King's College Hospital. Women, men or children can be referred by the police or refer themselves. The services offered at The Haven include forensic medical examination, first aid, emergency contraception, and preventative medication for HIV and STIs. The centre also offers follow-up for screening for STIs and for counselling.

There are plans to open sexual-assault referral centres at St Mary's Hospital in west London and at the Royal London in east London in 2003.

The REACH centres in Newcastle and Sunderland
REACH (Rape, Examination, Advice, Counselling, Help) offer free, confidential counselling, advice, support, information and forensic examinations to women and men, aged sixteen and over, who live in Northumberland and Tyne and Wear and who have suffered rape or sexual assault as an adult (i.e., who were aged sixteen or over when they were assaulted).

The Star Project in West Yorkshire
Star (Surviving Trauma After Rape) provides a confidential support service for women and men aged over fourteen years within West Yorkshire who have been raped or sexually assaulted as an adult. Staff are happy to help, whether or not people decide to report to the police. The project can be contacted in three ways: via the police, via the telephone helpline or by asking another person to phone on your behalf (for example, a relative, a partner, a friend, your GP or social worker). An initial-support worker can visit men and women at home to provide emotional and practical support for a six week period. Following this, the project can arrange for professional counselling and/or long-term practical help through a local Victim Support scheme. If you choose to report to the police, the project offers a case-tracking service to ensure you are kept informed of the progress of any criminal investigation.

Juniper Lodge Sexual Assault Response Centre in Leicester
Opened in May 1999 and sited at Leicester General Hospital, Juniper Lodge provides support to survivors of rape and sexual assault in Leicestershire. Women and men over sixteen can opt for self-referral and can choose to have no police involvement. Survivors can call the Monday helpline or leave a message at any other time. Support workers deal with the answering-machine messages regularly.

Telephone and face-to-face support, providing updates on the progress of a case, information from specially trained police officers or a medical examination are all offered to callers. Project co-ordinator Sandra Woodward says, 'Men and women are offered a support worker, a fully trained volunteer, who calls to arrange a support session for a few days after the assault. Up to eight sessions are offered at whichever frequency suits the person. After this we can make a referral to counselling, if that's what the person feels would be useful.' There is full disabled access at the lodge and literature in different languages, as well as an interpreting service and support workers with language skills. Callers are able to ring on someone else's behalf and give information about an attack anonymously.

The Safe Centre in Preston, Lancashire

This centre deals with cases of sexual assault and/or rape for women, men and children across Lancashire. It was set up in August 2002 and is on the site of the Royal Preston Hospital, so is close to Accident and Emergency and Genito-Urinary Medicine services. There is a trained crisis counsellor available round the clock, every day of the week, who can provide help and/or set up an examination. During office hours, he or she is available by phone or in person at the centre, and, outside those times, can be reached by telephone. There is also a trained nurse available to cover sexual-offence examinations. Carolyn Barrett, centre manager and a nurse with 25 years' experience, has been trained in the US as a nurse examiner. The Safe Centre is only the second SARC in the country to offer this service, following the St Mary's pilot scheme (see page 146).

The Shelford Suite at Addenbrooke's Hospital, Cambridge

The Suite is currently based in Accident and Emergency (although it is hoped there will be a purpose-built unit in the future) and provides a 24-hour service, also using St Mary's in Manchester as its model. There is an examination room and an interview room and any medical needs can be met due to its location. There is an arrangement with the Genito-Urinary clinic for staff to visit victims in the suite. At present, all referrals come via the police or Accident and Emergency, but there are plans to recruit crisis workers, so self-referral is also possible. There are also plans to start training nurses in forensic examination. It is hoped that eventually the same service will be offered in hospitals across the region.

'We have a huge area, which means that some victims wishing to use this centre would need to travel many miles, perhaps using a far-from-reliable public transport system,' says DI Chris Ford of Cambridgeshire police. 'By rolling out the service for the whole county, we provide the same response to rape now being found in many city-centre SARCs. This is our way of adopting an urban model for our rural community.'

Victim Support

'We receive calls from men and women who have been raped who are at any stage in the process – whether it has just happened or whether it occurred years ago,' says Gill Gridley of Victim Supportline. 'We take quite a lot of calls from people who have never told anybody about it.' The options that the Supportline would explore with a caller who had been raped might include:

*talking to a close friend or family member

*checking out their physical well-being and, if there were concerns, the Supportline would encourage the person to seek treatment, for example, at her GP or Accident and Emergency department

*contacting, or letting the Supportline contact, the caller's local Victim Support scheme

*contacting another voluntary agency, for example, a rape, support group

* giving general information on police procedures if someone was considering whether or not to report a rape to the police

* exploring the caller's safety, particularly if she had been raped within her relationship, and perhaps looking at the possibility of going into a refuge

'If the caller who had been raped was a child, we would contact social services on his or her behalf,' says Gill Gridley.

'It can take some callers quite a long time to decide what to do. During that period they may ring us quite a lot and we will continue to be there for them. Someone may be receiving help from their local victim-support scheme or rape centre and ring us to have someone to talk to when they're maybe not around. We are open longer hours than many local agencies.'

The National Association of Services for Male Sexual Abuse Survivors (NAMSAS)

The association can provide the service closest to you that can support male survivors of child or adult sexual abuse and rape.

Survivors UK

This organisation has been providing information, support and counselling since 1986 for men who have experienced sexual abuse and/or rape. There is a national confidential helpline for survivors which also supports their families, partners and friends. It also offers one-to-one counselling and group counselling. The Survivors UK website provides a National Register of Male Sexual Assault Counsellors. Go to 'NRMSAC' for a list of accredited counsellors.

General practitioners, accident and emergency or genito-urinary medicine clinics

If you go to your local hospital you do not have to identify yourself.

The morning-after pill and/or pregnancy testing can be obtained from a family-planning clinic, your GP or a genito-urinary medicine clinic (at most hospitals). Pregnancy-testing kits are also available at some rape and sexual-abuse centres or you can buy one from a chemist. Tests for STIs can be carried out at a GU clinic. Most hospitals have these.

STIs are easily and successfully treated if detected at an early stage. The thought of being tested can be daunting but it can be reassuring to know that you are free from infection, or that you are having any necessary treatment started quickly. You can also have blood taken for HIV/AIDS testing at any GU clinic. The virus can take up to three months to show up, so you may be advised to repeat the test later. Tests are free and confidential. You don't have to give your real name, if you wish, and results will not be sent to your GP. Many GU clinics will also provide pre- and post-test counselling.

Social services
All social services have an emergency team that operates at night. It can respond to calls and involve the police, if required. Social services, Rape Crisis, Women's Aid, Refuge and the Citizens' Advice Bureaux can all offer advice and support to women needing to be re-housed.

Citizens' Advice Bureaux
Advice can be given about health checks and emergency contraception, reporting rape to the police and compensation. The Citizens' Advice Bureaux should also be able to help sort out possible problems with employment, housing and any other practical issues arising from the attack. Bureaux advisers can give information about organisations that offer counselling and other support. All advice is free, confidential and independent.

The choice to report
Philippa

It's not until you've been through it yourself that you realise just how difficult the situation is. Most people still seem to assume that it's the woman who has asked for it – either in the way she was dressed, her personality or whatever. So when it happens to you, you want to keep it to yourself.

Reporting a rape

According to the British Crime Survey 2000, which looked at all rapes experienced by women over the age of sixteen, approximately 20 per cent reported the crime to the police. In *Cosmopolitan*'s 2001 sex-crimes survey, only 27 per cent of respondents who had been victims of rape reported the offence to the police.

Everyone should be able to make their own decision about whether to report a sexual assault to the police or not. Police training and practice in the area of rape has improved enormously in recent years. There is now a better chance than ever before that you will be taken seriously, treated sensitively and with respect, and that you will be kept informed of the progress of the case.

If you do report the crime to the police, it does not mean that you will have to go to court or see the attacker again. You may decide to report and then not to go ahead with the case or the Crown Prosecution Service may decide there is not enough evidence to proceed. But the offence will still be recorded. If you decide to report, it is best to do so as soon as possible after the attack. But some reports come many years after a sexual assault.

'There is no time limit to reporting any crime, especially rape,' says DCI Richard Walton of Project Sapphire. 'The chances of conviction obviously diminish with time but it should not stop people reporting.

'We get a lot of historical rapes reported and encourage victims to come forward even if it is historical – if only for advice and counselling.' (See 'New techniques and cold case reviews', later in this chapter.)

Reasons women give for not reporting

In the 2001 *Cosmopolitan* survey, one in seven said this was because they were too scared or too young, one in ten because the offender was a family member or because they felt no one would believe them. Two in three respondents told a relative or friend.

According to the 'Australian Women's Safety Survey' conducted by the Bureau of Statistics in 1996, reasons for not reporting forced sex include:

*not acknowledging or naming the event as rape oneself

*thinking the police/others will not define the event as rape

*fear of disbelief

*fear of blame (especially if alcohol or drugs were involved)

*distrust of the police/courts

*fear of the court process and public disclosure

*fear of family/friends knowing

*fear of further attack/intimidation

*threats by the offender/his family or friends

*divided loyalties in cases involving current/ex-intimates and family members

*language/communication issues for disabled women and migrant women

Primary reasons for deciding to report to the police were given as:

*doing it automatically/its seeming the right thing to do

*wanting to prevent attacks on others

*wanting to prevent further attacks on oneself

*a desire for justice/redress

*someone else making the decision

Factors that increased the likelihood of reporting were:

*the offender was a stranger

*the use of force

*injuries

*location – it was a public place or in the context of a break-in

*the woman's informal network supported her

Several studies have shown that friends are the most likely people to be told and if they communicate strongly that what happened was not the woman's fault, this increases reporting.

Lynne Harne says it is still a lottery for women whether they are treated sympathetically by the police. 'Reports coming into the Federation about police response across the country show that it is by no means even. If you don't fit the framework of a "real rape", formed by the myths around rape, you may not be taken seriously.'

The most recent study to explore police responses, in 1999, involved interviews with women and with police officers. Women who were not happy with their first contacts with the police referred to not being believed and being dealt with by male officers as strong factors in their lack of satisfaction. Several police chaperones (a chaperone is a police officer attached to an individual's case to support her through police and/or court proceedings) commented that CID officers did not believe victims. A third of the police interviewed also estimated that at least a quarter of all reports were false. Delayed reports and date rapes featured in this observation.

But the study found that most victims were positive about police response. A female officer being present, the use of unmarked cars and being believed and reassured all contributed to this sense of satisfaction.

The Metropolitan Police's Project Sapphire began in January 2001 and is claimed to be the most comprehensive reform of rape investigation ever undertaken by the police. It has launched dedicated, 24-hour sexual-offences investigation teams in 30 of the 32 London boroughs. Front-desk staff in police stations are also being trained in how to talk to and respond to rape victims.

Project Sapphire's Richard Walton wants women to report all offences: 'The vast majority of indecent exposure is not reported. But many offenders start with minor indecency, like flashing, and then move on to more serious crimes. And although sex crime involving people who know each other can be difficult to prove, we urge women to report it. We are finding links between men who commit this type of offence and who attack strangers in the street. But without a woman reporting it we can't build up a case on someone. If we don't know what's happening generally, we can't improve the situation. Not reporting means the offender could be getting away with it consistently.'

Your choices

After a rape or sexual assault you have many options:

*Telling no one and doing nothing or confiding in someone you can trust but doing nothing.

*Asking the police to investigate the crime immediately, letting a doctor examine you and talking to a police officer – telling him or her as much as you can about what happened.

*Having a sexual-offences medical examination but not talking to the police yet. The forensic evidence (for example, samples of the attacker's clothing or blood) that the doctor finds can be sent to the police, with your agreement, and may be enough for them to find who the criminal is and if they have committed any other crimes. You may choose to speak to the police later.

*Having a medical examination and allowing the forensic evidence to be sent to the police with the information you choose to give (for example, you don't have to tell them who you are). You may choose to speak in more detail to the police later.

*Having a medical examination but no information being passed to the police. You may change your mind about this later.

*Giving details of the crime but not having a medical examination. You may choose to give more details or to have an examination later.

*Having medical treatment (for example, a test for STIs or treatment of injuries), but choosing not to have a medical examination and not to speak to the police.

*Going for counselling or seeking help from a support organisation by phone or in person.

You can change your mind at any time. But remember that the best forensic evidence from an examination is collected within seven days of the crime.

You may choose to make an allegation of rape or serious sexual assault either anonymously or by identifying yourself:

*at a hospital

*at a doctor's surgery

*at a sexual-assault referral centre

*by telephone from your home

*at the front counter of a police station

*through a third party

You may be advised not to go to the toilet or eat or drink until a sexual-offences examiner has examined you. This can be distressing if you want a hot drink or to smoke or you need the toilet. But now many first-response police teams have early-evidence kits, which contain a single mouth swab and a container for taking urine. This ensures effective and quick recovery of forensic evidence that can be lost due to time delays between reporting and a medical examination.

Reporting to the police

Sexual assault of adults is dealt with by a senior detective. Victims will have contact with this detective but will often have most contact with a police officer with special training in this area, known by many names, including a chaperone, a victim liason officer, a SOLO (Sexual-Offences Liaison Officer) or a SOIT (Sexual-Offences Investigation Training) officer.

This officer will tell you about police procedure, will accompany you to a medical examination, will take your statement and will keep you informed of developments in your case, such as whether the attacker is arrested, held on remand or granted bail. Sexual abuse of anyone under seventeen is dealt with by the Child Protection Unit. Assault by a partner or ex-partner may be dealt with by the Domestic Violence Unit.

Do not take any, or additional, alcohol or drugs before you go to report. This might be used against you in court. You have the right to take someone with you for support, to take along or ask for an interpreter if English is not your first language or you have a hearing or speech impairment and to ask for a female police officer and a female doctor (but bear in mind one or both may not be available). You can also leave the police station or medical examination at any time.

You should not wash, shower or take a bath until you have had a medical examination. But if you have, you can still press charges. It's a good idea to take a change of clothes to the examination, as the police may keep the clothing you were wearing when you were attacked, including your underwear, for evidence. If you haven't done this, other clothing will be found for you. The examination may take place in a special room at the police station, at a victim-examination suite or at a sexual-assault referral centre.

Will you get a female doctor if you have a medical examination?

The Home Office report 'Speaking up for Justice' recommended that, 'Victims (both male and female) of rape or serious sexual offences should have a realistic choice of being examined by a female doctor.' But in practice this choice is not always there.

St Mary's Sexual Assault Referral Centre in Manchester has, with Home Office support, piloted a scheme using the skills of a trained forensic nurse to carry out the victim forensic examination. This has been shown to reduce the waiting time for a daytime examination, as forensic physicians may have other commitments in general practice or hospital medicine.

'The forensic nurse conducts the examination, documenting any injuries and collecting samples,' says Bernie Ryan. 'Then when the police request a statement, the nurse provides a statement of findings, while a senior forensic physician makes a statement of interpretation based on those findings.

'We are lucky at St Mary's that we have ten long-standing forensic physicians but there is generally a problem recruiting and retaining female forensic physicians to conduct such examinations.

'The forensic nurse we have complements our forensic team. At the present time, nurses have not got the necessary experience to provide expert opinion. This may change with experience and further training. Forensic-nurse examinations may assist in the collection of early evidence and provide daytime cover for examinations.

'Our experience is that the role of the forensic nurse enhances the services to clients. And if this system is adopted countrywide it could make a real difference to victim care and to evidence in court.'

The forensic medical examination

You are traumatised after an assault but if you feel able to have an examination, then at least the evidence is stored, however you decide to proceed. Remember that this examination can provide evidence that is viable for forensic purposes only up to seven days after the rape. The purpose is to see if you need medical attention by checking and recording injuries and to look for and collect evidence that might identify the assailant.

Forensic gynaecologist and sexual-offences examiner Dr Ruhi Jawad has examined nearly 500 women, men and children who have alleged a sexual offence at The Haven, a sexual-assault referral centre in Camberwell, London. 'If the area you are in has no sexual-assault referral centre, then you may be taken to a GP's surgery, a police station or an exam suite in another building,' she explains.

The Association of Police Surgeons have set up rigorous guidelines for any doctor carrying out sexual-offences examinations. 'Many sexual-assault referral centres have developed similar guidelines for their practitioners,' says Dr Deborah Rogers of the Association. 'But any forensic medical examiner can download our guidelines from our website. We are always looking at ways to improve the forensic medical services available to victims of sexual assault.' It is hoped that standardisation of examinations will make evidence-gathering more efficient and consequently strengthen the cases of victims.

Information you should and should not give before, during or after an examination

*If you are asked how many times you have been pregnant, don't answer this. Say instead how many children you have. If you provide information about terminations and/or miscarriages, this can be used by the defence in court.

*Don't say you have been in prison.

*If you are a prostitute do not say this specifically. Perhaps you are officially unemployed, maybe you work part-time or you may be a mother. You can say these things instead.

*You should be asked if you have had sex with anyone else in the past two weeks. Answer this fully. The examiner will need to be aware of the source of all DNA on the swabs. If you withhold information this may be used by the defence if your case goes to trial. You should also say if a condom was used as condom lubricant can be detected on swabs.

Genital injuries

'One of the biggest misconceptions,' says Dr Jawad, 'is that there will always be physical and/or genital injuries when someone has been raped. I would say that the majority of women I see do not have genital injuries. But their absence does not mean they have not been raped. I am often called to give evidence in court and the defence always bring this issue up. They say, There were no injuries because she was aroused, her vagina was lubricated. But I always stress that there is always lubrication in the vagina of any woman who has passed puberty. Injuries depend on the degree of force used by the rapist. But because there are all kinds of ways in which a woman may be coerced – perhaps she genuinely fears for her life or that of her children – a rapist may have no need to use undue force.'

St Mary's Sexual Assault Referral Centre in Manchester is carrying out research into examination findings with GPs. 'We are looking at injuries following consensual sexual intercourse,' says Bernie Ryan. 'We hope that eventually we will be able to create a baseline, a clear idea of what occurs following consensual sex, that we can use for comparison with evidence following a sexual-offences examination in court.'

What you might encounter during a sexual-offences examination

It is up to you whether or not you have the examination and you can halt it at any time.

Your reactions to the examination will depend on very many factors but any reaction you have is normal.

It may be distressing for you to have a male, rather than female, examiner. If your examination is very soon after the attack, you may be in shock and feel quite numb to the experience.

You could find yourself reacting when the examination becomes intimate. Maybe you will experience fear, you might cry or you could feel extreme physical tension when being touched or looked at 'down there'.

The strength of your reaction may shock you but the examination is simply triggering your body to 'remember' the rape. There are suggestions later in this chapter that you may find helpful in supporting you through an examination.

The intimate part of the physical examination will last only minutes and is a small part of the overall examination, coming later in the process.

The police will brief the doctor on when and where the assault took place and who the suspect is. Information on age and ethnicity can help the doctor assess, for example, the risk of HIV. If it hasn't been done already, a mouth swab will be taken from you and you may then have a drink.

Whatever you reveal to the doctor may also be revealed in court and no counselling should be offered to you at this point. It can be regarded as directing the witness. This applies only if you choose to proceed and your case reaches trial. Although the police officer will be present during the examination, he or she will be behind a screen.

Before the physical examination
The brief details given to the doctor by the police officer will be read to you. You need only confirm these are correct. It saves you having to go through the traumatic account again.

The doctor will ask for details of the assault to help guide the examination – for example, of bruising or the taking of swabs. Questions might include:

Was there physical abuse? Did the attacker use lubricants? Was oral penetration attempted or achieved? Was there ejaculation? Was a condom used? Was there anal penetration? Did he ask you to give him oral sex? Were objects inserted into the vagina or anus? Did he kiss you and if so where? Did he bite you?

You will be asked about your general medical history. If you have had a hysterectomy or other gynaecological surgery, for example, this will change the anatomy of your genitalia and the doctor should be made aware of this.

The doctor will ask about your sexual and obstetric history – when you last had sex, if you were using contraception, how many children you have, how the deliveries went (an episiotomy – when you are cut to help deliver the baby – can, for example, leave scarring). You will need to make the doctor aware of any allergies you have to medications.

You will also be asked for a detailed history of your drug and alcohol consumption for the three days around the assault. It is best if you tell the truth about this. It will show up in blood and urine samples anyway. And if there is a discrepancy between what you say and the test results, this could, again, be used by the defence.

There can be a lot of questions but your answers may provide the police officer with information that can be passed on to the investigating officer – even while the examination is in progress – which might enable a suspect to be arrested.

The physical examination
This should take between 15 and 30 minutes, depending on the extent of injury. Your clothes may have been collected beforehand or the doctor may have to pass them to the police officer during the examination.

You and the doctor will continue to be screened off from the police officer. There may possibly also be a forensic nurse present to assist the doctor.

The doctor will begin by documenting the injuries on your body. Bruises will be described by size, colour and whether they are bleeding, etc. Swabs will also be taken, which may include saliva, pubic hair and/or semen. Washing before the examination can remove this evidence.

Photographs of injuries sustained in the attack may be taken at a later date. You can request a female photographer.

Your blood pressure and a blood test will be taken. Many people are nervous about blood tests but not having them is another point the defence may pick up on – did you have something to hide?

The genital exam follows. If you were penetrated vaginally then just a vaginal examination will be carried out. This will include a general overview of the area as well as internal samples. If only anal penetration is alleged, then you will still have a vaginal examination as semen can sometimes trickle through.

You may experience discomfort but the doctor should go slowly and gently. And the internal examination may reveal injuries that need immediate attention. 'Of course it is distressing to have a genital examination after a sexual assault but if you do decide to proceed with your case it is vital in capturing forensic evidence,' says Dr Jawad.

If there are facilities available to take a bath or to have a shower, you may use these now.

You may be asked to return the next day as some bruising is not obvious straightaway. Before you leave, the doctor will discuss emergency contraception and sexually transmitted infections. You may be asked to return for a check-up at the genito-urinary clinic at the hospital. If your assault is considered high risk, you could be offered drugs for HIV, which, if it is present, will treat it immediately. You might also be given a Hepatitis B and/or a tetanus vaccination.

When all the evidence has been packaged and the paperwork sealed, you will be able to leave. The evidence will be sent to a forensic laboratory for testing.

The whole thing will take about two hours.

The police may also take fingerprints to distinguish your prints from any others in an effort to identify the attacker. They will be destroyed once the case is complete.

Forensic testing

Forensic case work may take several forms: body-fluid examination, submissions for DNA testing, toxicology tests – for example, on blood and urine for alcohol and/or drugs – and tests for lubricants. Exhibits are taken from scenes of crime (including the clothing the victim was wearing) in order to try to establish what has happened, when it happened and where.

'We are trying to demonstrate that an allegation can be supported,' says Mary Newton, serious-sexual-offences officer for the Forensic Science Service in London. 'But whilst we can, for example, demonstrate that there are body fluids, we can't tell the jury if they are there as a result of consent or not. We describe how a garment looks – if buttons are missing, the feet of a zip are missing, if there are grass stains. But we can also do reconstruction tests on similar garments to see if damage is consistent with forcing and so on. Yet we are not routinely being asked to demonstrate damage – and it is that which might be more important when it comes to the issue of consent.'

Results can take a considerable amount of time to come back. Workloads in laboratories across the country can vary enormously but the forensic-science service in London quotes approximately 100 days for serious sexual-assault cases. Mary Newton explains, 'In certain circumstances we can prioritise and fast-track samples. Persistent young offenders need to be processed within three weeks and suspects in custody within 48 hours. If it is a stranger offence then the police are trying to find something to help their investigation. They don't want another one to happen overnight. If they can put a DNA sample on the national database quickly and get a name we do all we can to help them with that.

'We always encourage the police to inform us with regard to changes of circumstances, new court dates, arrested suspects and so on and we endeavour to meet these deadlines. We are trying to develop fast tracking of all sexual-offences samples. But until then, whatever the circumstances, as we complete any work we normally phone the information through so the officer involved in the case may be able to put the complainant's mind at rest.'

New techniques and cold case reviews

For stranger rapes, all exhibits – for example, clothing, weapons and so on – and DNA samples are stored for a minimum of 30 years.

'Cold-case reviewing is very important,' says Richard Walton. 'We are going back over stranger-rape cases from as long ago as fifteen years and applying new forensic techniques to get DNA from exhibits. It may be that a person who has not reported previously was raped by someone we are looking for for a different crime. So even if there is no forensic evidence (that is to say it is historical) the victim could still give verbal evidence which could help convict a serial offender.'

A revolutionary DNA technique has been developed by researcher Dr Ian Findlay, of the Australian genome research facility at the University of Queensland. Typical DNA finger-printing requires from 200 to 500 cells to produce enough material for a fingerprint but he has managed to take DNA fingerprints from single cells with an accuracy of 10 billion to one. When the breakthrough was announced in October 2002, cases before the Australian courts were already using the technology. Dr Findlay says the technology eliminates the problems of contamination because while normal profiles are taken from an aggregate of cells – some of which may come from different people – the new system relies on the evidence contained in one cell alone. Michael Strutt, an expert in forensic science and formerly of the Australian rights group Justice Action, said the system could be a breakthrough in rape cases, where forensic scientists often have trouble telling which part of the DNA profile came from the perpetrator and which from the victim.

The statement

Initial questioning should be brief and confined to: what has happened, when and where it happened and who was involved – that is, enough information for the police to take immediate steps, if necessary. These might include detaining the suspect and identifying the place(s) the assault took place, so exhibits, such as clothing, bedding or weapons, can be collected.

Your full statement will be taken in the days following the attack. This can take several hours but the process is usually broken into a few sessions. There will be detailed questioning, which may be demanding, so ask for breaks whenever you need them.

The police should record as evidence all comments made by the complainant to any other person as soon as possible. These comments might include details of the rape, where and when it happened or a description of the rapist; details that the survivor may not be able to recall later, or that may be recalled in a different form for the police statement. Other people's observations of the survivor's emotional reaction are also important. Any of these recorded details could provide essential evidence. This is one of the few circumstances where hearsay evidence will be accepted by a court.

Fearing disbelief, victims of rape sometimes try to embellish their accounts or conceal wrongdoing in order to make themselves appear more 'believable' to the police. But it is important that nothing be concealed or left unclear.

You should read your statement carefully when you have finished. Your statement and those of the witnesses will provide the main evidence to support the police investigation and any subsequent prosecution. It will be used in court – if you and the CPS decide to proceed – so accuracy is important. Copies will be made available to the alleged offender's defence lawyers if the matter goes to trial. But, although the statements must record the victim's and witnesses' addresses, these won't be handed over to the defence – unless the information is crucial to the offence.

Identifying the suspect

If you or other witnesses are able to identify the suspect, you may need to look at photos of potential culprits or help a police artist draw a sketch. You may also have to attend an identity parade or a voice identification may be tried. An identification line-up may be difficult for you as it obviously involves the chance that you may see your attacker again. But you will be protected by a one-way screen and will not be seen by anyone in the line-up. You can take someone with you for support.

No crime and no further action

For a rape to be 'no crimed', by the police there must be substantial reasons for believing that the allegation is false. Examples of this might be:

* if the victim admits it is false and makes a statement to that effect

* when medical evidence, forensic evidence or the account of an independent witness substantially contradicts, rather than supports, the allegation

*when there is substantial evidence that the victim is suffering from delusions or making the allegation for some inappropriate purpose (psychiatric impairment or alcohol/drug dependency is not the same as suffering from delusions)

If a victim withdraws an allegation because she does not wish to pursue a prosecution, then this is classed as 'no further action' and is recorded as an 'undetected rape'.

Evidence

The police have powers to arrest and search a suspect and to take possession of his property. He will be interviewed at length and will normally have a right to legal advice. But there are restrictions on how long he may be held. When the police have enough evidence, they must decide whether to charge the suspect. If they do charge, the police pass the case on to the CPS.

The alleged offender will be released on bail or 'remanded in custody' (held in a police station or prison to appear before the magistrate's court). Both the police and the courts can grant bail. This must be granted unless the alleged offender is likely to disappear, reoffend or threaten the witness. Conditions may be imposed on the bail – that the alleged offender must appear at a police station at specified times, live at a specific address or keep away from a location or the victim. Anyone who fails to comply with the conditions can be arrested and bail may be revoked. The court must give reasons for granting bail to someone charged with serious sexual offences.

If bail is refused and the alleged offender is remanded in custody, the remand must be renewed at a magistrate's court hearing at least every 28 days. If, during one of these hearings, the court grants bail to someone previously held in custody, the court should inform the police and give details of any conditions that are imposed. The police should in turn notify the victim and witnesses.

A case will be continued by the CPS only if there is sufficient evidence to provide a realistic prospect of conviction and it is decided that prosecution will be in the public interest. If the charges are dropped or substantially altered by the CPS, they should write to you and offer to meet you to explain their decision.

If the crime results in injury, loss or damage, the police should give you a form to complete so the court has enough information to be able to make a compensation order, if the offender is convicted. A compensation order is in addition to any claim the victim may make under the criminal-injuries compensation scheme. But the value of any compensation order awarded by the court may be deducted from any award made under that scheme.

Cases may not be pursued due to 'insufficient evidence'. A suspect may not have been found or there may have been a delay in reporting, for example, which might mean there is little evidence other than the word of the complainant and the denial by the defendant. The CPS might also feel that prosecution is not in the public interest. Only approximately one-third of all cases of rape reported to the police are proceeded with.

One study showed that cases involving under-16s and over-45s and those where there are additional levels of violence are the most likely to result in both a charge of rape and referral to the CPS for prosecution. But the study also notes that at least half of acquaintance rapes, gang rapes and rapes involving women with learning disabilities are not referred to the CPS.

Cases involving acquaintances are more likely to be 'no crimed' by the police. Those involving intimates, such as husbands or partners, are more likely to be designated 'no further action' or discontinued by the CPS.

Research carried out with judges and barristers for the Home Office in 1999, and on barristers in a separate study in 2000, point to a belief in the professions that acquittals are the result of an increase in 'weak' cases being prosecuted. 'Weakness' here seems to refer to cases that cannot be described as 'real rape', that is to say, those that involved a stranger and a weapon and which took place outside. It has been suggested that this view must have an impact on the CPS and their decisions about whether or not to proceed with a case.

In Scotland

When the police have collated all the evidence, a report is given to the procurator fiscal. The procurator fiscal decides whether or not there is enough evidence to prosecute the accused. You may be asked to attend a precognition interview with the procurator fiscal, who will go through your evidence with you. At this interview, you can ask any questions you may want answered.

The decision whether or not to prosecute, and for what crime, is in the hands of the public prosecution service and the foundation for this decision should be that prosecution is in the 'public interest'. Police investigate and report to the procurator fiscal, who is allowed to make the decision to prosecute with complete discretion. This means the decision is not open to review or question, particularly by the female complainer.

In Northern Ireland

In Northern Ireland, cases can be prosecuted by the police or the director of public prosecutions. If it is the latter, a decision is made following the submission of a police investigation file and also possibly consultation with the alleged victim and an independent barrister. After careful consideration, it may be decided not to proceed with the case. The alleged victim may put any feelings she has about this decision in writing. The director of public prosecutions will then explain the decision.

To report or not to report

'"Letting him get away with it" is a phrase I hear again and again from women who both have and haven't reported,' says Susan Van Scoyoc. 'In my experience, women who don't report feel bad about themselves, that they've been weak, that they've let him get away with it. The women who don't report seem to regret it later.

'If you do report there will possibly be a further period of severe stress involving an examination, investigations, even a trial. But long term you will probably feel better about yourself for taking a proactive approach. Even if the case reaches court and the guy is not convicted, with all the repercussions that can have on you personally, even those women say that despite his getting away with it at that stage they feel that at least they did all they could.'

9

Rape on Trial

A woman who has survived rape and whose case reaches court will not necessarily be called as a witness. But when women do find themselves in this position, many describe feeling victimised all over again, that the experience of being cross-examined by the attacker's defence barrister is like a second rape. In fact, in a recent study, more than three-quarters of women whose cases went to court said that they felt they were the ones on trial.

Before you take the stand, it can be helpful for you to know something about the court process and where you fit into it. And there is a lot you can do to prepare yourself for giving evidence in court. For example, while attempts have been made in recent years to avoid women being questioned about their past sexual history, you should be aware that loopholes may be found.

There are matters beyond your control that may lead to outcomes that you will find hard to deal with. Plea bargaining is one example and is described later in this chapter, on page 177. Even a conviction with a sentence of several years is not without difficulties. If you were living with the man who raped you there may, for instance, be repercussions for you financially or on your family. You may also feel nervous when the attacker is up for parole or due to be released.

Nevertheless, you should remember that there are many agencies in place to support and inform you. And that laws continue to change to improve women's experiences in court. Many areas of the criminal-justice system are also being closely looked at in order to make real changes to the conviction rate for rapists.

Clinical psychologist Linda Blair suggests that women facing giving evidence should go to see a skilled counsellor, their GP or a therapist. 'Pick someone to whom you feel comfortable talking. You need to get used to talking about what happened. The more you talk, the more you'll be able to speak coherently and put your experiences into a logical order. If you don't do this, you might find you go on the witness stand and you're overwhelmed by fear and unable to express yourself.

'If you don't communicate well, it gives the defence more opportunity to harass you. You need to give yourself the chance to tell it like it was.'

The magistrate's court

All criminal proceedings involving adults begin in the magistrate's court. The first stage in court proceedings is the committal hearing. The defendant will be brought before the magistrates, where it will be decided if there is enough evidence for the case to go forward to the crown court for a full trial. No oral evidence is given at committals, so you should not be required to attend. Witnesses do not have to appear for every hearing held in connection with the case – their evidence will be reserved for the trial.

The crown court

How long will it take before the case goes to trial?

Once a case has been transferred to the crown court, there will be a 'plea and directions' hearing. If the accused pleads not guilty, the CPS will prepare the case for a full jury trial. In rape cases this can take about six months but may take up to a year.

If the plea is 'not guilty', it is important that anyone who will be called as a witness leave the court as soon as the words 'not guilty' are spoken so that they do not hear the discussion of the future trial. If they stay, they can no longer be called as a witness and could be seen to have influenced other witnesses – including the victim – with the information they have heard. Any witness who fails to leave may therefore jeopardise the trial.

The witness service

As a victim of rape, you are considered as a witness for the prosecution, so it is useful to know about the witness service. 'The service is in every crown and magistrates' court in England and Wales,' says Andrew Buckingham of Victim Support, the national charity that helps people cope with crime and that runs the service. 'It is free and confidential and provides emotional support and practical information about court proceedings for prosecution and defence witnesses, as well as relatives and friends. It is available before, during and after a hearing or trial.

'There are a number of ways you can access it,' Buckingham explains. 'Via the Victim Supportline (see page 203), through your local branch of Victim Support, the police station, or simply by looking up the number for the witness service in your local phone book. They are always based in the court building.'

The witness service will normally contact you after it has been confirmed that you are required to give evidence in court. The CPS, solicitors and police can also refer people.

The service can provide a pre-trial visit to the courtroom. 'This gives you the chance to see who sits where and to find out the roles of key court personnel,' says Buckingham. The service also provides quiet, and in many cases separate, waiting areas for defence and prosecution witnesses.

How will I know when the trial is due to start?

The police should tell you and any other witnesses when you will be needed to give evidence in court. You should be given an early warning that the case may be listed within four weeks. But the exact date depends on how long other cases take and is sometimes notified to participants only the day before. When a date is set, the trial will be listed in the defendant's name and allocated to a specific courtroom. Witnesses are entitled to claim travel expenses for attending court and associated costs, such as childcare and loss of earnings, from the CPS.

Can I take someone with me to court?

You don't have to attend court alone. You can take a friend or relative. But note that if you are attending the central criminal court, also known as the Old Bailey, in London, you will have to give notice in advance that you are bringing someone with you.

Take any information you have about the case – for example, the name of the police officer dealing with your case, if you know it, and the letter asking you to attend court, if you receive one. You could also take something to read or do – you may have to wait a long time for the case to be called – and money to cover the costs on the day, for example, car parking and refreshments.

Legal representation

In a prosecution the CPS acts on behalf of the general public interest and prosecutes in the name of 'the Crown', not the victim. It can be very hard for a victim to understand that they are not party to the case in the same way that the defence – the alleged attacker – is.

As a victim, you do not have the right to your own legal representation

This places you at an immediate disadvantage compared with the defendant. He can choose his own legal team who have his interests at heart. You must rely on the CPS and you are not allowed to meet the Crown barrister prosecuting your case until the morning of the trial. Research has shown that two-thirds of prosecution barristers don't even say 'Hello' to the woman before she goes into court.

You have no special rights other than in your role as a prosecution witness who, depending on how the case proceeds, may or may not be called to give evidence. And because you are not involved in your own case, except as a witness, you have no power to refuse consent to any plea bargaining (see page 177) that can take place.

Specialist prosecutors

In the UK, a rape complainant may meet with someone from the CPS prior to their trial but the barrister prosecuting the victim's case in court will have minimal, if any, contact with the complainant prior to the trial. As has already been pointed out, they may introduce themselves to the victim only on the day.

In the US, however, the lawyer from the District Attorney's office meets with the complainant as soon as she reports the crime. This lawyer will then be involved in the police investigation and will also prosecute the case if it reaches trial. Statistics prove that this system leads to higher conviction rates.

The 2002 report on rape cases by the inspectorates of the CPS and the police says that, in deciding whether to forward a rape complaint to the CPS, police express subjective, critical views about complainants' characters as witnesses. And prosecutors, who are not specialists in rape, review cases looking for weaknesses, not for ways of strengthening them.

The report recommended that the way forward was for all allegations of rape to be reviewed by prosecutors who have received specialist training in the handling of sexual offences. It also suggested that all cases where a prosecutor is contemplating dropping, or substantially reducing, the prosecution case should be seen by, and/or discussed with, a second prosecutor before the final decision is made.

The media
Newspapers, magazines, radio and television are all prohibited from identifying victims, witnesses or defendants involved in court cases if they are under the age of eighteen or if they are the victims of rape or sexual assault. (In fact, from the moment a victim has reported a crime of sexual violence to the police, her identity is protected from publication.) Judges have the power to restrict reporting by the media of derogatory assertions made by the defence against the victim's character. Journalists are allowed to draw sketches in court but not of the victim.

There has been a lot of discussion about extending anonymity to defendants who are acquitted of rape offences. It has been argued that it is unfair to protect victims but not defendants because the stigma of unsubstantiated rape charges is great. But others argue that parallels should not be drawn between victims and defendants in rape cases. Instead, comparisons need to be made between defendants in rape cases and defendants in other types of case. The stigma of being unfairly accused of murder or major fraud might be just as great but there has been no call for anonymity in these situations.

Who will be in the court?
The judge and the prosecution and defence barristers, the clerk, the police, ushers, the jury and the press will be present. Your family, friends, relatives and/or colleagues and members of the public may also attend.

When the trial begins
There may be a delay before proceedings start – if an earlier case takes longer than expected, for example. All crown courts have separate waiting areas, which reduces the risk of victim and witnesses coming face to face with the accused or his

family and friends. Anyone not called to give evidence may sit in the public gallery for the duration of the trial. Witnesses cannot go into the courtroom, including the public gallery, until they have given evidence.

The jury will be sworn in. The defence and prosecution barristers can reject or accept members of the jury.

If the defendant pleads guilty, then you will have no further part in the proceedings as it will only remain for the judge to either pass sentence there and then or adjourn the case while he obtains relevant reports.

If the defendant pleads not guilty, then 'plea bargaining' may be initiated by the prosecution or defence team. Under the Victims' Charter, the prosecution must take your views into account before a decision is made. The defendant will, for example, be asked if he is willing to plead guilty to a lesser charge – perhaps sexual assault rather than rape – and this would guarantee a conviction. But remember that although you will be consulted on this matter, the ultimate decision on whether to accept a plea is with the prosecution. You should also be aware that if the defendant does plead guilty to a lesser charge, you will not have to give evidence in court and the attacker's punishment will be less severe.

The prosecuting counsel, acting for the CPS, will outline the details of the alleged crime and call their witnesses. Each witness is questioned by the prosecuting counsel and then the defending counsel. Each witness may be re-examined on any points raised and the judge may also ask questions. The police officer in charge of the case, and medical and forensic experts may also be called to give evidence. Forensic evidence may be looked at.

If the defence wishes to call any witnesses, they will be questioned first by the defence and then by the prosecution. The defendant cannot be compelled to give evidence but will be the first defence witness to be called if the defence decide to do this. Other defence witnesses may include an alibi witness, character witnesses and experts presenting psychiatric or medical reports.

When all the evidence has been presented, if the defence believes that the prosecution has failed to present enough evidence for the jury to convict, it may submit that there is 'no case to answer'. The jury will be sent out of the courtroom while the judge decides. If the judge agrees, the jury will be called back in and directed to acquit the defendant and the case will be closed. If the judge disagrees, the trial will continue.

The prosecution and the defence will summarise the case. The judge will address the jury, highlighting relevant issues on which the case rests and explaining points of law. This may include that they can find the accused guilty of a lesser charge. The jury leaves the court to consider its verdict.

The jury must be convinced that the prosecution has proved that the crime has been committed by the accused and that the accused intended to carry it out. The standard of proof is high and the jury must be satisfied 'beyond reasonable doubt' before the accused can be found guilty.

If the members of the jury are unable to reach a unanimous verdict, they will be called back and the judge will advise them about making a majority decision on which at least ten members agree. If they are unable to do this, they will be discharged. The CPS may apply for a retrial.

If the verdict is not guilty, and if there are no further charges, the accused is freed. This does not necessarily mean that the jury believes the accused is innocent but rather that the defending counsel cast sufficient doubt on the case to make a guilty verdict unsafe.

Giving evidence
The prosecution will ask you to state what happened and try to establish certain facts. The defence, on the other hand, will probably try very hard to discredit your account of events. Be prepared for rigorous questioning.

Special facilities may be available in the court to help witnesses give evidence. For example, interpreters can be arranged for witnesses who do not speak English. The Youth Justice and Criminal Evidence Act 1999, Section 17 (1), refers primarily to youths but acknowledges that adults in certain circumstances can be regarded as vulnerable witnesses. Adult victims of sexual offences are defined as 'intimidated' and as such are eligible for 'special measures'.

'Special measures' can be applied for at a 'special measures' hearing. They are: screens, evidence by live link, evidence given in private, removal of wigs and gowns, video-recorded evidence in chief (meaning video evidence is the main but not the only form of evidence given by the victim), video-recorded cross-examination or re-examination and examination of the witness through an intermediary.

The only measure that cannot be applied for by adult victims of sexual offences (victims over seventeen) is video-recorded evidence in chief. They will need to give a statement too. But Phase 22 of the new act will come into effect in July 2003 and will allow police to video interviews and to use the videos as evidence in court for all victims of rape. Police will need to apply to the CPS for these measures and there will be special measures hearings. The measures will not automatically be granted.

Past sexual history

It is stated in the Sexual Offences Act of 1976 that there be restrictions on the cross-examination of a victim about any sexual experience with a person other than the defendant. Further restrictions appear in sections 41–3 of the Youth Justice and Criminal Evidence Act 1999, in relation to evidence or questioning about a victim's sexual behaviour beyond the circumstances of the alleged offence. This, it says, should only be done at the judge's discretion.

But, in practice, it appears that instead of limiting sexual-history evidence to a minority of cases where it is directly relevant to the facts of the case, many loopholes are used by the defence to try to discredit the woman's character in relation to her previous relationships.

In a 2000 study of senior barristers by Jennifer Temkin, it became clear that they employed a deliberate strategy of undermining the woman's personality in court. Two-thirds of the women whose cases went to court said they were directly asked about whom they'd had sex with or other questions that implied they were promiscuous. And Canadian research found that jurors who heard evidence of the woman's past sex life were less likely to find the defendant guilty and that their belief was in direct proportion to the amount of this kind of material revealed, even if the complainant denied it all.

The report for the CPS and police inspectorate in 2002 recommended that clear instructions be given to the prosecution that offensive and seemingly irrelevant questioning should be challenged and that inappropriate cross-examination about previous sexual experiences should be tackled. Home Office research into the operation of the provisions of section 41 of the Youth Justice and Criminal Evidence Act is at the preliminary stage and is expected to be published in spring 2004.

Legislation came into force in Scotland in November 2002, bringing it into line with the rest of the UK, which meant that men accused of rape and sexual assault could no longer question their alleged victim in court. But it went further than in England and Wales by stipulating that a victim's sexual history could be brought up by defence lawyers only if the defendant's previous history of sexual offences is disclosed to the jury. Under the Sexual Offence (Procedure and Evidence) (Scotland) Act, defence lawyers have to tell the court at least fourteen days before trial if they intend to bring up the victim's sexual history. If they do this, the Crown has the automatic right to disclose any previous convictions for sexual offences to the jury.

She said 'No' but I thought she meant 'Yes'

The white paper, 'Protecting the Public', unveiled in November 2002, addressed the crucial issue of 'honest belief'.

Currently, if a man believes that a woman consented to sex he cannot be guilty of rape, even if his belief was unreasonable (the 'honest belief' defence). In deciding whether or not a man believed that a woman was consenting to sex, the jury is instructed to have regard to the presence or absence of reasonable grounds for such a belief.

The defence of 'honest belief' allowed him to argue that he thought the woman was consenting, even though she said no or struggled. He could claim she was sending mixed messages on the basis, for example, that her sexual history suggested something different from what she was saying and how she behaved.

In the Home Office review 'Setting the Boundaries', in 2000, it was recommended that 'A defence of honest belief in free agreement should not be available where there was self-induced intoxication, recklessness as to consent, or if the accused did not take all reasonable steps in the circumstances to ascertain free agreement at the time.'

Under the suggested reforms outlined in the white paper, the defence will be allowed 'honest belief' only in cases where the belief was reasonable. If there is reasonable doubt about whether the woman consented and the man failed to take reasonable steps to ensure she was willing, he will be guilty of rape.

A new statute will list a range of circumstances in which consent is presumed to be absent. These include situations where the victim was:

*subjected to force or fear of force

*put in fear of serious harm to herself or another person

*abducted or unlawfully detained

*unconscious

*unable to communicate consent because of physical disability

*had agreement given by a third party

The law would make it clear that sexual activity with someone incapable of consenting because of a learning disability or mental disorder would be an offence.

If the prosecution proves one of those circumstances existed, it will be for the man to prove the woman agreed to sex.

Can I find out if the defendant has done this before?
Under plans unveiled in November 2002 in the Criminal Justice white paper, 'Protecting the Public', judges will be able to allow jurors to hear about defendants' previous convictions and details of other 'bad character' evidence, where relevant. A woman who previously made complaints against a rape defendant could be called to give evidence, for instance, even if no action had been taken over the earlier complaints. So a man who has been repeatedly accused and acquitted of date rape may, for example, see former witnesses recalled in a later case. This rule will not be limited, as now, to cases where the defendant acted in a strikingly similar way each time.

Other issues that can be used against women alleging rape in court
*Medical records. Many women have had their records called before the court – for example, to call their mental health into question, to point out drug or alcohol use or even to talk about genito-urinary infections. Often these issues are raised when they bear no relation to the case at all. They are simply used to humiliate the woman and discredit her in the eyes of the jury.

*Counselling. The fact that a woman is in counselling is used by the defence to claim she has been rehearsed in her evidence.

*Criminal-injury compensation. Women are asked if they have applied for this and, if they have, it is suggested they are making a wrongful accusation of rape for financial gain.

*Sexual abuse as a child or previous sexual assault. The defence may raise this and imply the woman is unstable or hates men as a result.

*Abortion. If a woman has had an abortion, either as a result of the rape or in the past, the defence may use this information to try to discredit her.

*Lack of injuries. Yet research has shown that clear external or internal injuries occur in only about a quarter of reported rape cases.

*Behaviour. There are considered to be certain common-sense and natural responses to a crime. People often expect victims to be upset and angry. Yet research evidence shows that there are a range of responses from victims. They may be extremely distressed but it is also likely that a victim's reaction will be quiet and controlled. The latter does not mean the victim is any less affected by the rape. (For information on what it is advisable to say during a medical examination, see page 159.)

Women's experiences on the witness stand, from Eileen Calder of the Rape Crisis and Sexual Abuse Centre, Northern Ireland

Mary

I was in the witness box for two whole court days. It was the worst two days of my life. His barrister passed my underwear round the jury, they were all fellas about the same age as the rapist... He [the defence barrister] asked me if I had a thing about men in uniforms [Mary's rapist told her, falsely, that he was a police officer, which was why she trusted him. She had worked in contract catering in a police station.]... He called me a liar and expected me to remember exactly where my right hand was and his left hand was every second of the rape. It was like going through it all again in slow motion with him telling you you were making it all up... He accused me of learning my statement off by heart with my counsellor. But the judge spoke up and asked me if counselling had helped me emotionally. That fairly sickened him... When the police surgeon showed him the picture of the bruises, four fingermarks and a thumb mark round my throat, he argued with this doctor that they were love bites. No matter what the doctor said he just kept saying it.

In the end the jury must have believed him. They let him off didn't they?... When he was giving his closing speech he walked over to the jury box and leaned on it like he was in the pub and said, You know what it's like boys, you buy these women a drink and a hamburger, drive them home for a kiss and a cuddle, they change their minds and then cry rape. Is it any wonder they let him off?

Lorraine

My barrister said at the meeting that there was no way they would try to imply that rape didn't happen or that I had sex with him willingly. My counsellor wasn't so sure and told him that. She was right in the end because his barrister accused me of making up the whole thing even though he started out by saying that he believed it was rape but that it wasn't his client. [The unusual knife which Lorraine described was found in the rapist's bedroom along with a packed bag and everything he was wearing that night washed, including his trainers]... He [the defence barrister] asked me if my vagina was wet or dry. I knew what he was getting at, I'm not stupid. But why did he ask me those things when he was saying I invented the whole story and that no rape had ever happened?... Then when I tried to explain the way he had me lying, and I said the sixty-nine position, he let on he didn't know what I was talking about and made some comment or other to the jury about me being well versed in the language of adventurous sex...

Other tactics used by this particular barrister were to suggest that Lorraine invented her story in order to get compensation. Like the defence in Mary's case, he also suggested she had rehearsed her story with counsellors. He suggested that she did not care about her baby, who had lain in the next room sleeping because she did not disturb him out of his sleep and bring him into her room after the rape. She found this even more upsetting than the sexual slurs he made on her character. It is important to remember that Lorraine was lying in her own bed at home when an armed intruder raped her.

Both women said that they felt they would never recover from the court case. This was attributed entirely to the defence barrister's cross-examinations. Both even used almost exactly the same words to describe their feelings. Lorraine: 'He's just as bad as the man who raped me and I hate him just as much.' Mary: 'I hate him. He made me feel exactly like the rapist did, but what he did was legal, legal abuse.'

How rape myths can affect a trial

According to Professor Liz Kelly's review in 2002 into the reporting, investigation and prosecution of rape cases, a report by the Scottish Executive published two years earlier showed how rape myths can 'amount to forms of prejudice which, if they come into play in a trial, result in the complainant being treated with a lack of respect and, in the worst cases, being humiliated.' These commonplace beliefs include:

*someone who has had sex with persons A and B is more likely to have it with person C *someone who is 'sexually promiscuous' has less right than someone who is not to choose whom they are sexual with

*someone who is 'sexually promiscuous' is generally less trustworthy, and therefore less likely to be telling the truth

*women have a tendency to 'lead men on' and are therefore to blame if men fail to resist their physical impulses

*When women say no they do not always mean it

*False allegations of rape and sexual assault are more common than false allegations of other crimes [this is not the case]

Few studies on the acceptance of rape myths have been done in the UK. But, Kelly points out, many have in the USA. 'Overall findings suggest that men are much more likely to have limited definitions of what constitutes rape and in simulations of jury decision-making these attitudes affect their behaviour.' In fact, says Kelly, one key US study showed that the acceptance of rape myths accounted for trial outcomes more accurately than any of the evidence presented in the case.

Another important study talks about the idea of 'real rape'. This is considered to be rape committed by a stranger, outdoors and involving weapons and injury. 'In reality,' says Kelly, 'these four conditions are rare.' But all rapes are measured against this and this has repercussions on decision making by police, prosecutors and judges and juries.'

When you're on the witness stand
The Rape and Sexual Assault Support Centre in London suggests:

*don't be afraid to ask for clarification if you are not sure about certain questions

* answer questions at your own pace

* if you do not feel comfortable answering certain questions then ask the judge if you can reject the question. Questions

relating to your past sexual history are allowed at the discretion of the judge

* if at any stage you feel overwhelmed, ask the judge for a short adjournment (break)

Karen Foulger of West Yorkshire Victim Support recommends that women:

*Stick to the facts. Don't feel you have to enhance or cover up what happened or what took place before the rape. Don't, for example, feel you should hide the fact you were drinking.

*See the judge as your best friend and pick two faces you like the look of in the jury to direct your answers to.

*Remember that it is the defence's job to get the best for his client. It is not personal, it is not him or her versus you. So you should try – and I know this will be incredibly difficult, but you should try – to stay as emotionally detached as you can.

After your evidence you can sit in the public gallery and see how the case develops. However, bear in mind that family and friends of the defendant may be there.

Mitigation
If the verdict is guilty, the court will be told about the accuser's previous conduct, including convictions. The defence may make a statement putting forward reasons why the sentence should be less severe than it might otherwise be. This may include his disputing facts raised by the prosecuting counsel or even attempting to criticise the victim's character.

Before sentencing
The judge can ask for a pre-sentence report to be prepared detailing the offence and the circumstances that led up to it. This should include an assessment of how the crime affected the victim, information about the offender, for example, previous offending and the liklelihood of reoffending, and an assessment of risk to the public.

Sentencing

Injury, use of weapons and repeated sexual offences are some of the factors that can be seen as aggravating the severity of a case. But, in certain rape cases, they can be used as a form of mitigation – where reasons are given for a sentence to be less severe than it might otherwise be.

'It has been our experience that judges often give lighter sentences when the rapist pleads guilty, using the reason that he wanted to spare his victim the trauma of giving evidence,' says Una Gillespie of the Rape and Sexual Assault Centre in Northern Ireland. 'Had he wanted to spare his victim trauma he would not have raped her in the first place.

'Also, there is no medical treatment available to "cure" rapists and abusers. The little therapy there is available seeks simply to control their behaviour. There is no reason why this therapy should not be carried out within the prison system. It should not be used as an excuse for non-custodial sentences.

'Rapists and child abusers only show "remorse" when they are caught and facing a prison sentence. At the centre we know from what our clients tell us that the only thing they regret is getting caught.'

In 1986, in response to public outrage at lenient sentences imposed by a number of judges in rape cases, Lord Chief Justice Lane issued new sentencing tariffs (the Billam Guidelines). With no mitigating circumstances, five years was the starting point with fifteen years for a campaign of rape. Where there were aggravating features, such as two or more rapists acting together, rape that takes place in the victim's home, rape coupled with the abuse of a position of responsibility or rape involving abduction and confinement of the victim, the starting point was set at eight years. Various mitigating factors were also outlined: that young offenders could claim special mitigation, pleading guilty could reduce the sentence and where the victim 'had behaved in a manner which was calculated to lead the defendant to believe that she would consent to sexual intercourse'.

The proportion of custodial sentences of at least five years for the substantive offence of rape nearly doubled between 1985 and 1987 – from 42 per cent to 79 per cent and for attempted rape it increased fourfold from 10 per cent to 40 per cent. And, in 2000, the average sentence for rape by an adult was seven years and four months.

However, since 1987, the length of sentences has decreased. According to research, there appear to be wide discrepancies in sentencing in different parts of the country, with sentences of less than three years or non-custodial sentences being far more likely to be awarded in some areas – despite the guidelines stating that sentences under three years are not appropriate for rape, even in cases with one or more mitigating factors. And, according to calculations in this research, 40 per cent of sentences in 1991 were of five years.

In May 2002 the sentencing advisory panel, the official body that advises judges on sentencing, said that judges seemed to have been passing lesser sentences when the rapist and his victim were known to each other. Yet this was not a mitigating factor under the Billam Guidelines. The panel's chairman, Professor Martin Wasik, said, 'Our advice to the court of appeal is that new guidelines should include a clear statement that "relationship rape" and "acquaintance rape" are to be treated by sentencers as being no less serious than "stranger rape".' The panel recommended that the starting point for a rape, five years in prison, should remain, with an eight-year starting point for rape of a child or other vulnerable person, gang rapes, rapes by some-one in a position of responsibility or with sexually transmitted disease and repeated rapes in the course of one attack.

Tara

I was abused as a child but have chosen not to report it. What's the point in putting myself through the pain and humiliation of a trial? I was on a jury of a man who was found guilty of eleven

*charges of sexual abuse on girls under fourteen. He had to
serve a maximum of four years in prison and a minimum of two.
How is that justice? I'm sure I'm not alone in my reasons for not
reporting sex crimes. Justice cannot be served in Britain today.
I am lucky to have a very positive outlook on life and I live by the
view that both good and bad things make you the person you
are. I have given myself a very good life and my justice is that
he has not ruined my life. That's more than the courts can do. If
the government want to protect women they should look at the
sentences given by the courts. Only more reasonable
sentences will encourage people to report crimes, thus keeping
dangerous men off the streets.*

Following sentencing

Witnesses can be reluctant to give evidence because they are
afraid the offender may 'get off' and come after them. But
witness intimidation is itself an offence. So if witnesses have
been intimidated after a trial that has resulted in the accused's
acquittal, that acquittal may be quashed and a retrial held. If
you are intimidated, you should tell the police or the CPS
immediately and, if necessary, ask for protection.

The CPS should tell the police if a guilty offender decides to
appeal either against his conviction or his sentence. If he does
appeal you will not become involved in this. The accused may
be allowed bail pending the appeal hearing. The police should
keep the victim informed about the date of the hearing,
whether bail is granted and the result of the appeal. If the
accused is found guilty and there is concern that the sentence
is too lenient, the victim, the CPS or the lawyer involved can
write to the attorney-general. If the attorney-general agrees,
the case may be referred to the court of appeal. This must be
done within 28 days of the sentence being passed.

Under the latest Victims' Charter, the probation service has
a responsibility to contact victims of sexual or violent offences
where the offender is sentenced to one year or more.

The probation service should explain the custodial process to the victim and ask if she wishes to be kept informed of any conditions to which the offender may be subject on release, such as where the offender is allowed to work, live or go. Any anxieties the victim has in this respect may be taken into account but the victim will not be asked to comment on whether the offender should be released and she will not be told where the prisoner is being held. If a victim receives unwanted contact from a prisoner or wants to know when he will be released, she can also call the prison service helpline (see page 212).

In Scotland
If the accused is to be prosecuted and is in custody, you may have to wait up to 110 days before he appears in court. But if he is on bail, you may have to wait up to a year after his first court appearance before the case is tried. However, he will be warned not to approach you and should you have any concern for your personal safety, contact the police immediately. The defence lawyer is entitled to an interview with you at this stage. If you feel you would like more information about this, you can contact the procurator fiscal. Cases of rape are always heard in the high court. Attempted rape or serious sexual assault may be dealt with either in the high court or in the sheriff court. There could be a jury present in the sheriff court. The difference between the two courts is the power they have for sentencing. As you are the chief witness you will not be legally represented in court. Members of the public may be cleared from the courtroom when you give evidence but there will still be a number of people left, including the accused. If the trial is heard in the high court and the accused is found guilty, there is no upper limit to the sentence. If the case is heard before a sheriff and jury, there is a maximum sentence of three years and if the case is heard before a sheriff only, the maximum sentence is six months. If the verdict is 'not proven', that

means there has not been enough evidence to convict the accused and he will be released. If he is found not guilty, he will be released. You cannot appeal against this verdict. If you report the crime to the police, you may be entitled to claim compensation from the Criminal Injuries Compensation Authority (see page 210).

In Northern Ireland

If the director of public prosecutions takes the decision to proceed with a case it can reach trial more quickly than in England and Wales. Committal proceedings and the arraignment process will take several months but if the alleged rapist pleads guilty then it will, on average, take a month from arraignment to the case reaching trial. As in England and Wales, the case would go to a magistrate's court before the crown court.

It is currently still possible for the accused to cross-examine the victim in court in Northern Ireland but there are plans for this to be abolished in late 2003. The maximum sentence for rape is life imprisonment.

Other legal options

Civil action

An injunction

An injunction requires a person to stop doing something. For example, a woman can apply for an injunction ordering her partner not to assault her or to enter their home. To break an injunction is not a criminal offence but is treated as 'contempt of court'. The police can enforce an injunction only if it has a 'power of arrest' attached to it (see page 107).

A civil claim

This can be brought by the victim against an offender for injury, property loss or damage. It should be noted that this is a separate remedy to making an application for compensation from the Criminal Injuries Compensation Authority (CICA).

Both this and a civil claim are the only civil options for obtaining compensation and any compensation from a civil claim will be deducted from compensation awarded by the CICA.

Liz Dux, a lawyer who has worked extensively with rape victims, says that you must bring a civil claim within six years of the offence. It can be a lengthy process 'and I only recommend bringing this action if you can show the person can afford to pay damages. If they have a job you may be able to get an attachment of earnings, where they pay you in small instalments. But you will incur significant legal costs which you will only get back, with damages, if you win.'

For criminal-injuries compensation claims, the test is one of balance of probabilities that the defendant committed the alleged act. Therefore a conviction in a criminal court is not a prerequisite. 'The time limit for criminal-injuries compensation is two years but it may be flexible, depending on the circumstances,' says Dux (see page 31).

But Dux cautions that you cannot apply for criminal-injuries compensation unless you've done everything you can to bring your alleged attacker to justice. 'This includes prompt reporting to the police, assisting them fully with their inquiries and giving evidence in court.

'Some victims like to go down the civil- or criminal-injuries compensation route because it can offer recognition that this happened and, because we are looking at the balance of probabilities, the burden of proof is less than in a criminal trial.'

But, Dux cautions, the civil- or criminal-injuries process can be as draining as a criminal case. 'And there is no guarantee of success.'

A private prosecution
It may be possible for a victim to bring a private prosecution against the alleged offender if the CPS decides not to prosecute a case. This must normally be brought within six months of the

crime and involves applying to a magistrate to issue a summons. This will be granted if the applicant has an arguable case with adequate evidence.

Whoever brings the private prosecution can conduct the case themselves and have a friend to help but professional legal advice should be obtained. The case has to be proved 'beyond reasonable doubt', as with a criminal case.

The CPS has the right to take the case over at a later date and, if it then considers that the prosecution is not in the public interest, the case may be discontinued. If the case goes ahead and the victim fails, she may have to pay the other side's costs, or even be sued for damages herself if it can be shown that the prosecution was 'malicious'. Even if the victim wins, the accused still has the right to appeal.

'Be aware that a private prosecution of any kind or making an application for compensation to the Criminal Injuries Compensation Authority could involve you seeing your attacker again,' says Liz Dux. 'The CICA can invite the alleged assailant for a meeting if there is a dispute over your eligibility to claim.

'Think carefully about what you are hoping to achieve. Talk to a lawyer about what you want, what it will cost and whether it is a worthwhile exercise.' And you should go to a lawyer with specific experience, recommended by a support agency for rape victims, by a Citizens' Advice Bureau or even the Law Society.

'You don't want to go through a two-year draining legal process only to be advised by your lawyer that you should pull out,' Dux warns. 'But if someone was not prosecuted and has a job you can do a lot of damage by pursuing a civil claim against him. People will find out, it will make his life uncomfortable.'

In civil cases, initial legal advice and assistance may be available to victims under the *green-form scheme*. This enables people with limited means in England and Wales to be granted up to two hours of a solicitor's time. Scotland and Ireland have separate schemes. Victims not eligible for this should enquire about a fixed-fee interview. Ask a solicitor if he or she offers this and what the fee would be for an assessment of your legal position. Law centres sometimes give free legal advice. Try the Citizens' Advice Bureau or Victim Support for advice on who might be able to help in your area. People with limited means have previously been entitled to apply for Legal Aid to fund the costs of legal advice and taking action in the civil courts. The Legal Aid Board is in the process of being replaced by the Legal Services Commission. This new agency will run two new funding schemes – the Community Legal Service for family and civil cases and the Criminal Defence Service for criminal cases.

Criminal-injuries compensation scheme

A victim can make an application to the CCICA for up to two years following a trial in which the accused was found guilty, but acquitted on a technicality, or if the criminal court does not award the victim compensation, or she can apply if the CPS decides to discontinue the case.

You may receive a payment for your own pain and suffering, whether mental or physical, and you may be able to claim a separate payment for loss of earnings or special expenses. You may also be able to claim a personal-injury award if you were present when someone very close to you was injured as a result of a violent crime and this caused you mental damage.

The CICA has a scale, or tariff, of payments with the current minimum amount of pain and suffering payable set at £1,000 and the maximum £250,000. You can apply for state compensation yourself but may find it helpful to seek legal advice. You will not be able to claim the cost of that advice from the CICA but you may be entitled to receive free intial legal consultation. Criminal-injuries application forms are available from the CICA (see page 210), police stations, Victim Support and Citizens' Advice Bureaux.

You should consider applying if you can answer 'yes' to both of these questions:

Have you been physically or psychologically injured because of a violent crime? Did the crime take place within the last two years?

Or if you can answer 'yes' to both these questions: Has your parent, child, husband, wife or partner died as the result of a violent crime? Did he or she die within the last two years?

Or yes to these four questions: Do you have a close relationship with another person who has been the victim of a violent crime? Were you present when the crime took place, or involved immediately afterwards? Did your involvment in the incident cause you a psychological injury? Did the crime take place within the last two years?

Compensation cannot be paid in the the following circumstances:

* the crime took place outside England, Scotland or Wales

*you suffered only a single minor injury, such as a black eye

*the crime took place more than two years ago, unless the CICA can still get enough information about what happened and there is a good reason why you did not apply before. The CICA say they will probably not accept a late application, unless you were injured as a child, your English is poor or you have a learning difficulty

*you were a victim of sexual abuse, or other sexual assault, which ended before October 1979, and you and the person who assaulted you were living together as members of the same family

*you were the victim of a road traffic accident, unless a vehicle was used deliberately to injure you

There are other things that may affect your claim. In assessing an application, the CICA normally ask the police for a report on the incident and the doctor or hospital that treated you for a report on your injury. There does not need to be a conviction for the CICA to pay compensation but it is important that you do what you can to help the police. For example, the CICA may ask if you reported the crime to the police or other authority as soon as possible after the incident; and/or if you helped the police investigate the case, for example, by making a statement or going to an identity parade; and/or if you told the police that you would be prepared to go to court and give evidence if the offender came to trial.

The CICA will refuse compensation, or reduce the amount it will pay, if you (or the victim in the case of injury that causes death) have a criminal record.

10

The Future

This book has not been about telling you what to do, the best way to live your life, the right way to respond to what happens to you. It is here to support, to inform and to guide you. What, if anything, you choose to do when it comes to personal safety is entirely your decision.

It has been argued that when so many women are raped by someone they know, it is pointless even to give advice on personal safety. But many experts agree that being aware of personal safety is empowering, it gives you confidence.

Research has demonstrated that thinking ahead and having confidence might keep you safe or enable you to eventually reach a safe place – whether or not you know the attacker, whether the incident is isolated or is part of long-term abuse.

You might be unaware of this advice, you might choose not to take it or you could do everything possible to guard your safety and still be raped. You could find yourself, or those close to you, being threatened. You may freeze from fear or from an instinct to survive.

Throughout this book it has been stressed that, whatever the circumstances around the rape, it is never your fault. There are precautions you can take, steps you can follow if you feel you are about to be raped, but this does not make you responsible if you are raped. It cannot be said often enough – the responsibility for rape lies with the rapist.

There is much left to do to educate and legislate about rape. There are too many people who think forcing someone to have sex might be OK in certain circumstances, and too many of us with a damagingly narrow view of what it means to be raped.

We are still seeing too many rape trials end with the rapist walking free. And we have a lot to do to improve support for survivors, whether or not they choose to report.

But, in the 2000s, rape has been high on the political agenda, there are plans to make dramatic changes to the laws to do with sex crime and the police have made vast improvements in their approach to the reporting and detection of rape.

And with sensitive policing, effective support services and an overhauled court system, it is hoped women will feel more able to explore their options after a rape, less fearful that they will be victimised all over again.

If you have been raped, it is understandable if you feel that it has changed your life, changed you so much that you are confused and desperate, that there is no hope.

Support can be helpful. You have to want it, to feel ready for it. But if you get support from those close to you, as well as from specialist individuals and groups, it can make a difference.

Nothing can take you back to being the way you were or get you to a point where you forget that rape or abuse happened. But you can move forward.

The way you are behaving and feeling is a response to what's happened in your life. You are experiencing trauma. But psychologists stress that trauma is learnt and that it can be unlearnt. You have survived something momentous but you can come through it positively.

There has recently been a particular focus on safety advice for women in relation to minicab rape, drug rape and the rape of women on holiday abroad. They are all areas in which the risk of rape is perceived to be increasing.

But we are all vulnerable. Whoever we are, whatever our age, whether we're overseas or at home, single and out clubbing or in a relationship. Greater awareness of the risks might make us safer. Knowing the options open to you if you're a rape survivor could make you stronger.

In these pages you can find both acknowledgement of your fears and of your rape. But you will not find pity. Because this book is about power. If you fear rape, it's about giving you power. If you have experienced rape, it's about helping return the power that's been taken from you.

This book is about leaving you with choices that can help you live the life you want to – with confidence.

Help

These pages are organised into sections, which are designed to guide you to the support you feel may suit you best. Each section is arranged in alphabetical order.

GENERAL SUPPORT

Edinburgh Women's Rape and Sexual Abuse Centre
Offers practical and emotional support to women and girls from age 12 who have experienced sexual violence (child sex abuse, rape or sexual assault) at any time in their lives.
Tel: 0131 556 9437 (Supportline)
Email: ewrasac@aol.com
Address: Edinburgh Women's Rape and Sexual Abuse Centre, PO Box 120, Brunswick Rd, Edinburgh, EH7 5WX

National Association of Citizens' Advice Bureaux
Provide free and confidential advice through local bureaux.
Tel: 020 7833 2181 or look in your local phone directory for your nearest branch.
Website: www.citizensadvice.org.uk

Rape and Sexual Abuse Support Centre (RASASC)
For women and girls over 13 who have been raped or sexually abused and will refer male victims on.

Tel: Helpline 020 8683 3300, open 365 days a year
Website: www.rasasc.org.uk
Address: PO Box 383, Croydon, Surrey, CR9 2AW

Rape Crisis Federation (Wales and England)
Call for your nearest rape-crisis group or to use the confidential
helpline at the largest provider of support services for women
who are adult survivors of sexual violence. Male survivors are
referred on but the RCF will support male partners of female
rape survivors.
Tel: 0115 900 3560
Website: www.rapecrisis.co.uk
Email: info@rapecrisis.co.uk
Address: Unit 7, Provident Works, Newdigate Street,
Nottingham, NG7 4FD

Rape Crisis Federation in Ireland
Website: www.rcni.net for a guide to the national network

The Refuge National 24-Hour Domestic Violence Helpline
Offers national support for victims of domestic violence.
Tel: 0870 599 5443

The Samaritans
Provides 24-hour support for people feeling depressed,
isolated or in despair.
Tel: (UK) 08457 909090
         (ROI) 1850 609090
Website: www.samaritans.org.uk
Email: jo@samaritans.org

Survivors of Lesbian Abuse
Offers support to women who have survived lesbian abuse as
a child or adult and/or women who feel they are currently
experiencing abuse.
Tel: 020 7328 7389

Victim Support (England, Wales and Northern Ireland)
The Victim Supportline and national association of Victim Support Schemes provide practical help and emotional support to victims and witnesses of crime.
Tel: 0845 3030900, 9 a.m.–9 p.m. weekdays, 9 a.m.–7 p.m. weekends, 9 a.m.–5 p.m. bank holidays
Website: www.victimsupport.org
Email: supportline@victimsupport.org.uk
Address: PO Box 11431, London, SW9 62H

Victim Support (Republic of Ireland)
Tel: (01) 8780870

Victim Support (Scotland)
Tel: 0131 668 4486; Helpline 0845 603 9213
Website: www.victimsupportsco.demon.co.uk
Address: 15–23 Hardwell Close, Edinburgh, EH8 9RX

Women Against Rape
Tel: 0207 482 2496
Email: war@womenagainstrape.net
Website: www.womenagainstrape.net
Address: Crossroads Women's Centre, 230A Kentish Town Road, London, NW5 2AB

Women's Aid Federation
Provides support and temporary refuge for people threatened by violence or abuse.
Tel: National 24-hour Domestic Violence Helpline 08457 023468; female translation service available.

COUNSELLING AND THERAPY

The British Psychological Society
Tel: 0116 254 9568
Website:www.bps.org.uk (go to 'Find a psychologist' for a register and directory of chartered psychologists across Britain).

Women's Counselling Service

Offer a helpline, face-to-face counselling and group work for women in the London area who have been sexually abused as children and/or have experienced or are experiencing sexual violence as adults.

Tel: 020 8572 0100, Mondays, 6.30–9 p.m. or leave a message 24 hours a day

Email: womenscounselling@zoom.co.uk

Website: www.womenscounselling.org

The Women's Practice

Tel: 01245 349072

Website: www.twp-psychology.com

(see also Sexual Assault Referral Centres and Victim Support in General Support)

SEXUAL-ASSAULT REFERRAL CENTRES (SARCS)

The Haven

Women, men or children can be referred by the police or can refer themselves. Services offered include forensic medical examination, first aid, emergency contraception, preventative medication for HIV and STIs, follow-up for screening for STIs and counselling.

Tel: 020 7346 3453.

Website: www.kingshealth.com/clinical/gum/index.htm

Address: Dept of Sexual Health at King's College Hospital, The Caldecot Centre, 15–22 Caldecot Road, London, SE5 9RS

Juniper Lodge

Telephone support, face-to-face support, updates on the progress of a case, information from specially trained police officers and medical examinations are offered to rape and sexual-assault survivors in Leicestershire. Women and men over 16 can opt for self-referral, choosing to have no police involvement.

Tel: 0116 273 3330 Helpline
Address: Lodge 1, Leicester General Hospital, Gwendolen Road, Leicester, LE5 4PW

The REACH Centres
Offer free, confidential counselling, advice, support, information and forensic examinations to women and men, aged sixteen and over, who live in Northumberland and Tyne and Wear who have suffered rape or sexual assault as an adult (i.e. who were aged sixteen or over when they were assaulted).
Tel: (Sunderland) 0191 565 3725; (Newcastle) 0191 212 1551, 8 a.m.–5 p.m. weekdays
Email: reach.sunderland@btinternet.com or reach.newcastle@btinternet.com
Website: www.reachcentre.org.uk
Address: The Ellis Fraser Centre, Sunderland Royal Hospital, Kayll Road, Sunderland SR4 7TP, or The Rhona Cross Centre, 18 Jesmond Road West, Newcastle on Tyne, NE2 4PQ

The Safe Centre
A trained crisis worker is available 24 hours a day, seven days a week. The centre provides support, counselling and sexual-offence examinations for women, men and children across Lancashire.
Tel: 01772 523344 (Helpline) or 01772 523949 (Counselling line)
Email: safe@lthtr.nhs.uk
Address: The Safe Centre, Royal Preston Hospital, Sharoe Green Lane, Fulwood Preston, Preston, Lancashire, PR2 9HT

St Mary's Centre
For female and male adults in Greater Manchester who have experienced rape or sexual assault at any time in their lives, the 24-hour services offered, regardless of whether a report has been made to the police, include telephone support, forensic

medical examination, emotional and practical support, one-to-one counselling for clients and their supporters, screening for HIV and sexually transmitted infections and support through criminal proceedings and compensation claims.
Tel: 0161 276 6515/6434
Address: St Mary's Hospital, Central Manchester Healthcare NHS Trust, Hathersage Road, Manchester, M13 OJH

The Star Project
Provides confidential support for women and men aged over 14 years within West Yorkshire who have been raped or sexually assaulted as an adult, whether or not a report has been made to the police. Support workers can visit clients at home, arrange professional counselling and/or long-term practical help.
Tel: 01924 298954 (Helpline)
Email: star@starproject.vianw.co.uk
Address: 4 Laburnum Road, Wakefield, WF1 3QP

SEXUALLY-TRANSMITTED-INFECTIONS SUPPORT

The National Sexual Health Informationline
Provides confidential information, advice and support about sexually transmitted infections, HIV and AIDS.
Tel: 0800 567123

Terence Higgins Trust
Offers help and advice for people affected by HIV and AIDS.
Tel: 0845 1221 200
Website: www.tht.org.uk
(see also *sexual-assault referral centres*)

SUPPORT FOR CHILDREN, PARENTS AND ADULT SURVIVORS OF CHILD SEXUAL ABUSE

Childline
Provides support for children or for any adult concerned about the welfare of a child.
Tel: 0800 1111
Website: www.childline.org.uk

Childline (for people calling in the Republic of Ireland)
Tel: 1800 666 666

Children First (formerly the Royal Scottish Society for the Prevention of Cruelty to Children)
Tel: 0131 446 2300
Website: www.children1st.org.uk

Childwatch
Offers free and confidential counselling for children and adults who have survived abuse.
Tel: 01482 325552
Email: info@childwach.org.uk
Website: www.childwatch.org.uk

Family Rights Group
Offers advice to families whose children are involved with social services.
Tel: 020 7923 2628.
Website: www.frg.org.uk

Irish Society for the Prevention of Cruelty to Children (ISPCC)
Provides support for any adult concerned about a child. If a person is under 18 and calling in the Republic of Ireland, the ISPCC suggests they contact Childline (listed above).

Tel: 003 53 16794944
Email: ispcc@ispcc.ie
Website: www.ispcc.ie

Kidscape
Founded in 1984 to prevent child abuse and bullying, Kidscape
has free booklets to help parents and children.
Tel: 020 7730 3300
Website: www.kidscape.org.uk

National Association of Services for Male Sexual Abuse Survivors (NAMSAS)
(see *Support for men*)

National Children's Homes (NCH Action for Children)
Tel: 020 7704 7000

National Society for the Prevention of Cruelty to Children (NSPCC) in England, Wales and Northern Ireland
Tel: 0808 800 5000; for a copy of the Child Witness Pack call
020 7825 2500
Website: www.nspcc.org.uk
Address: NSPCC Publications Department, 42 Curtain Road,
London EC2A 3NH

ParentLine Plus
Provides a 24-hour telephone support for parents.
Tel: 0808 800 2222
Website: www.parentlineplus.org.uk

Rape Crisis Federation
(see page 202)

Survivors of Lesbian Abuse
(see page 202)

Youth Access

Provides information and advice for young people and the names of counsellors in the local area.
Tel: 020 8772 9900

The Zero Tolerance Charitable Trust

An independent national organisation that campaigns for the prevention of male violence against women and children.
Tel: 0131 221 9505
Email: zerotolerance@dial.pipex.com
Website:www.zerotolerance.org.uk

SUPPORT FOR MEN

National Association of Services for Male Sexual Abuse Survivors (NAMSAS)

Tel: 07949 994886
Email: info@namsas.org.uk
Website: www.namsas.org.uk (to find the service closest to you)
Address: NAMSAS, PO Box 2470, London, SW9 6WQ

Rape Crisis Federation (Wales and England)

Supports male partners of female survivors
(see page 202)

Survivors UK

Supports and provides resources via a national confidential helpline for men who have experienced any form of sexual violence; also supports families of survivors, partners and friends. One-to-one and group counselling is also offered.
Tel: Helpline 0845 1221201 (Tuesday and Thursday 7 p.m.–10 p.m.)
Website: www.survivorsuk.org.uk – go to NRMSAC (National Register of Male Sexual Assault Counsellors) for a list of accredited counsellors.

CRIMINAL-JUSTICE SUPPORT

Compensation Agency Northern Ireland

Government agency responsible for administering criminal-injuries compensation in Northern Ireland.

Tel: 028 90 249944

Website: www.compensationni.gov.uk

Address: The Compensation Agency, Royston House, 34 Upper Queen St, Belfast, BT1 6FD

Criminal Injuries Compensation Authority (CICA)

Provides information about the Criminal Injuries Compensation Scheme and provides and aids with the completion of personal-injury or fatal-injury application forms.

Tel: 0800 358 3601

Website: www.cica.gov.uk

Address: CICA, Tay House, 300 Bath Street, Glasgow, G2 4LN

Crown Prosecution Service (CPS)

Government agency responsible for prosecuting people in England and Wales charged by the police with a criminal offence.

Tel: 020 7796 8500

Email: enquiries@cps.qsi.gov.uk

Address: CPS Correspondence Unit, 50 Ludgate Hill, London, EC4M 7EX

Police Complaints Authority

Statutory agency responsible for the investigation of serious complaints against the police.

Tel: 020 7273 6450.

Website: www.pca.gov.uk

Victim Support (England, Wales and Northern ireland)

The Victim Supportline and National Association of Victim Support Schemes provide practical help and emotional support to victims and witnesses of crime in England, Wales and Northern Ireland.

Tel: (see page 203)

(For republic of Ireland see page 203)

LEGAL SUPPORT

Association of Child Abuse Lawyers (ACAL)

Tel: 01923 286888

Email: info@childabuselawyers.com

Website: www.childabuselawyers.com

Address: PO Box 466, Chorley Wood, Rickmansworth, Herts, WD3 5YU

The Bar Council

The regulatory and representative body for barristers in England and Wales.

Tel: 020 7242 0082

Website: www.barcouncil.org

Children's Legal Centre

Tel: 01206 873820, weekdays 2–5 p.m.

Faculty of Advocates

Body of independent lawyers in Scotland.

Tel: 0131 226 5071

Website: www.advocates.org.uk

The Law Society

Professional body for solicitors in England and Wales.

Tel: 020 7242 1222

Website: www.lawsoc.org

The Law Society of Northern Ireland
Tel: 028 90 231614
Website: www.lawsoc-ni.org

The Law Society of Scotland
Tel: 0131 226 7411
Website: www.lawscot.org.uk

The Prison Service Victim Helpline
For victims of crime or those related to a victim who are worried about the prisoner's release or have received unwanted contact from a prisoner.
Tel: 08457 585112, 9 a.m.–4 p.m. weekdays.

The Rights of Women Advice Line
For legal advice.
Tel: 020 7252 6577, Tuesday, Wednesday and Thursday 2–4 p.m. and 7–9 p.m.

Scottish Child Law Centre
Provides advice on how Scottish law relates to children.
Tel: 0131 667 6333 (Advice line), Monday, Tuesday, Wednesday and Friday 9.30 a.m.–4.30 p.m., Thursday 6–7.30 p.m.

The Solicitors' Family Law Association
Tel: 01689 850227.
Website: www.sfla.org.uk (go to 'Find an SFLA solicitor').

PERSONAL SAFETY

Crime Concern Trust
Voluntary agency working to prevent crime and create safer communities.
Tel: 01793 863500

Liz Clark at Women's Self Defence
Tel: 07967 243667
Website: www.womens-selfdefence.co.uk
Address: PO Box 614, Enfield, Middlesex, EN3 6ZH

PERSONAL ALARMS

The Suzy Lamplugh Trust's Personal Shriek Alarm has an ear-piercing shriek to shock and disorientate an attacker, giving you vital seconds to get away. A cheque for £9 (including £1.50 p&p) is payable to SLT Training and Resources Ltd
Address: PO Box 17818, London, SW14 8WW

The Walk Easy 15-333 Trident Multi-Function Personal Attack Deterrent has a simultaneous loud siren and an emission of a cloud of foul odour, combined with an 'invisible' ultra-violet tracer which clings to an attacker's skin and clothing. Traces are still visible under a police ultra-violet lamp after up to seven days of regular washing of the skin. Ten police forces, including the Metropolitan Police, have these alarms available to buy. They can also be purchased from:
Tel: 01223 892 623; fax: 01223 893 880
Website: www.walkeasy.ltd.uk
Address:Walk Easy Ltd, Unit 3, The Grip Industrial Estate, Hadstock Rd, Linton, Cambridge, CB1 6NR

The Suzy Lamplugh Trust
Provides personal safety guidance which aims to enable people to prevent problems or to deal with, defuse or avoid a confrontation rather than engage in a last-minute defence.
Tel: 020 8392 1839
Website: www.suzylamplugh.org

Transport for London
To check the licence of a minicab firm in London.

Tel: 020 7222 1234
Website: www.tfl.gov.ukpco

WOMEN-ONLY CAB FIRMS IN LONDON

Ladybirds
Tel: 020 8295 0101

LadyCabs
Tel: 020 7254 3501

Ladycars
Tel: 020 8981 7111

Ladycars Ltd
Tel: 020 8655 1918

SUPPORT FOR TRAVEL OVERSEAS

The Association of British Travel Agents (ABTA)
Tel: Helpline 0901 2015050
Website: www.abta.com

Foreign and Commonwealth Office
For up-to-date advice on travel overseas.
Tel: 020 7008 1500
Website: www.fco.gov.uk or for information on problems
affecting your safety in over 200 countries visit
www.fco.gov.uk/knowbeforeyougo

Lonely Planet
Factsheets are available for women travelling abroad.
Tel: 020 7841 9000
Website: www.lonelyplanet.com

Bibliography

Reference

Ahmed, K, 'Women angry as "rapists go free". The *Observer*, 30 July 2000.

Baird,V, 'Rape in Court'. London, Association of Labour Lawyers, 1998.

Bargen, J & Fishwick, E, 'Sexual Assault Reform: A National Perspective'. Canberra, Office of the Status of Women, 1995.

Buckingham, Andrew, 'Coping in Court' in the *Police Review*. London, Jane's Information Group, 2002.

Burton, S & Kitzinger, J, 'Young People's Attitudes Towards Violence, Sex and Relationships'. Child, Woman and Abuse Studies Unit, University of North London and The Media Research Unit, Sociology Dept, University of Glasgow for the Zero Tolerance Charitable Trust, Glasgow City Council, Manchester City Council and Fyffe Council, 1998.

Campbell, R, 'The role of work experience and individual beliefs in police officers' perceptions of date rape: an integration of quantitative and qualitative methods'. *American Journal of Community Psychology*, 23:2, pp. 177–249, 1995.

Chambers, G & Millar, A, 'Investigating Rape'. Edinburgh, HMSO, 1983.

'Childhood Matters', Report of the National Commission Inquiry into the Prevention of Child Abuse. London, The Stationery Office, 1997.

George, W et al., 'Self-reported alcohol expectancies and post-drinking inferences about women'. *Journal of Applied Psychology*, 25:2, pp. 164–186, 1995.

Greenfield, L, 'Sex Offences and Offenders: An Analysis of Date Rape and Sexual Assault'. US Dept of Justice, Bureau of Justice Statistics, 1997.

Harris, J & Grace, S, 'A Question of Evidence? Investigating and Prosecuting Rape in the 1990s'. London, Home Office, 1999.

'The Haven Report'. May 2000–January 2002.

Heenan, M & McKelvie, H, 'Towards changing procedures and attitudes in sexual assault cases' in Easteal, P (ed.), *Without Consent: Confronting Adult Sexual Violence*. Canberra, Australian Institute of Criminology, 1993.

Her Majesty's Inspectorate of Constabulary (HMIC) and Her Majesty's Crown Prosecution Service (HMCPSI), 'A Report on the Joint Inspection into the Investigation and Prosecution of Cases Involving Allegations of Rape'. London, 2002.

Jordan, J, 'True "Lies" and False "Truths": Women, Rape and the Police'. New Zealand, PhD thesis, Victoria University of Wellington, 2002.

Kelly, Professor Liz, 'A Research Review on the Reporting, Investigation and Prosecution of Rape Cases'. Her Majesty's Crown Prosecution Service Inspectorate, London, 2002.

Kersetter, W, 'Gateway to justice: police and prosecutorial response to sexual assaults against women'. *Journal of Criminal Law and Criminology*, 81: pp. 267–313, 1990.

Kersetter, W & Van Winkle, B, 'Who decides: A study of the complainant's decision to prosecute in rape cases'. Criminal Justice and Behaviour, 17:3, pp. 268–283, 1990.

Kilsby, P, 'Aspects of Crime: Children as Victims'. Home Office, London, 1999.

Konradi, A, 'Preparing to testify: rape survivors negotiating the criminal justice process'. Gender and Society, 10:4, pp. 404–432.

Lees, S & Gregory, J, 'Rape and Sexual Assault: A Study of Attrition'. London, Islington Council Police and Crime Prevention Unit, 1993.

Lisak, D & Miller P M, 'Repeat Rape and Multiple Offending Among Undetected Rapists'. Violence & Victims, 17, pp. 73–84, 2002.

Maguire, M & Corbett, C, 'The Effects of Crime and the Work of Victims Support Schemes'. Aldershot, Gower Publishing Ltd, 1987.

New South Wales Standing Committee on Social Issues, 'Sexual Violence: Addressing the Crime. Legislative Council', Parliament of New South Wales, 1996.

Painter, Kate, 'Wife rape, marriage and law: survey report, key findings and recommendations'. Manchester University Department of Social Policy and Social Work, 1991.

Patterns of Crime Group, 'British Crime Survey'. Home Office Research Development Statistics Department', 2000 (annual).

'Rape in America: A Report to the Nation'. National Victim Center and Crime Victims Research and Treatment Center, 1992.

'Redressing the Balance: Cross-Examination in Rape and Sexual Offence Trials – A Pre-legislative Consultation Document'. Scottish Executive, 2000.

Reeves, H, 'The treatment of rape and child victims as witnesses of crime'. Leeds, Anne Spencer Memorial Public Lecture, 18 February 1997.

Royal College of Psychiatrists, 'Rape'. Council Report CR47, 1996.

Rumney, P, 'When rape isn't rape: sentencing in cases of marital and relationship rape'. *Oxford Journal of Legal Studies*, Vol. 2, 1999.

Schafran, L, 'Maiming the soul: Judges, sentencing and the myth of the non-violent rapist'. *Fordham Urban Law Journal*, 20, pp. 439–453.

Sexual Offences Unit, 'Protecting the Public'. Home Office, London, November 2002.

Shapland, J, Willmore, J & Duff, P, 'Victims in the Criminal Justice System'. Aldershot, Gower, 1985.

Sinclair, H & Bourne, L, 'Cycle of blame or just world: effects of legal verdicts on gender patterns in rape-myth acceptance and victim empathy'. *Psychology of Woman Quarterly*, 22, pp. 575–588, 1998.

'Speaking Up For Justice'. Home Office, Interdepartmental working group on the treatment of vulnerable or intimidated witnesses in the criminal justice system, 1998.

Stekettee, G & Foa, E B, 'Victims in the Criminal Justice System'. Aldershot, Gower Publishing Ltd, 1977.

Sturman, P, 'Drug Assisted Sexual Assault'. London, Home Office, 2000.

Temkin, J, 'Plus ça change?: reporting rape in the 1990s'. *British Journal of Criminology*, 37, pp. 507–528, 1997.

Temkin, J, 'Prosecuting and defending rape: perspectives from the bar'. *Journal of Law and Society*, 2000b.

Temkin, Jennifer, 'Reporting rape in London: a qualitative study'. *Howard Journal of Criminal Justice*, 38:1, pp. 17–41, 1999.

Williams, L, 'The classic rape: When do victims report?' *Social Problems*, 31, pp. 459–487, 1984.

Women's National Commission, 'Growing Up Female in the UK'. The Cabinet Office, London, 1997.

Women's National Commission, 'Violence Against Women'. The Cabinet Office, London 1985.

'The Victim's Charter'. London, Home Office, 1996.

Victim Support, 'Women, Rape and the Criminal Justice System'. London, Victim Support, 1996.

Books

Brown, B, Burman, M & Jamieson, L, *Sex Crimes on Trial: The Use of Sexual History Evidence in Scottish Courts*. Edinburgh, Edinburgh University Press, 1993.

Corbett, C & Hobdell, K, *Victims of Crime: A New Deal?* (eds Maguire, M and Pointing, J). Milton Keynes, Open University Press, 1988.

Easteal, P, 'Rape in marriage: has the licence lapsed?' in Easteal, P (ed.), *Balancing the Scales: Rape, Law Reform and Australian Culture*. Sydney Federation Press, 1998.

Estrich, S, *Real Rape: How the Legal System Victimizes Women Who Say No*. Boston, Harvard University Press, 1987.

Frazier, P & Seales, L, 'Acquaintance rape is real rape', Koss, M & Cleveland, H, 'Stepping on toes: social roots of date rape lead to intractability and politicization', in Schwartz, Martin D (ed.), *Researching Sexual Violence Against Women: Methodological and Personal Perspectives*. USA, Sage Publications, 1997.

Gregory, J & Lees, S, *Policing Sexual Assault*. London, Routledge, 1999.

La Free, G, *Rape and Criminal Justice: the Social Construction of Sexual Assault*. Belmont, California, Wadsworth, 1989.

Mooney, Jayne, 'Revealing the hidden figure of domestic violence', Harwin, Nicola & Barron, Jackie, 'Domestic violence and social policy: Perspectives from Women's Aid', Lees, Sue, 'Marital Rape and Marital Murder', in Hanmer, Jalna & Itzin, Catherine (ed.) with Quaid, Sheila and Wigglesworth, Debra, *Home Truths About Domestic Violence: feminist influences on policy and practice*. London, Routledge, 2000.

Russell, D, *Rape in Marriage*. Indianapolis, Indiana University Press, 1990.

Spackman, Philippa (ed.), *Victim Support Handbook: Helping People Cope With Crime*. London, Hodder & Stoughton, 2000.